KHARISMA NUGROHO
FRED CARDEN
HANS ANTLOV

LOCAL KNOWLEDGE MATTERS

Power, context and policy making in Indonesia

POLICY PRESS SHORTS RESEARCH

First published in Great Britain in 2018 by

Policy Press
University of Bristol
1-9 Old Park Hill
Bristol
BS2 8BB
UK
t: +44 (0)117 954 5940
pp-info@bristol.ac.uk
www.policypress.co.uk

North America office:
Policy Press
c/o The University of Chicago Press
1427 East 60th Street
Chicago, IL 60637, USA
t: +1 773 702 7700
f: +1 773 702 9756
sales@press.uchicago.edu
www.press.uchicago.edu

© Policy Press 2018

The digital PDF version of this title is available Open Access and distributed under the terms of the Creative Commons Attribution-NonCommercial 4.0 license (http://creativecommons.org/licenses/by-nc/4.0/) which permits adaptation, alteration, reproduction and distribution for non-commercial use, without further permission provided the original work is attributed. The derivative works do not need to be licensed on the same terms.

British Library Cataloguing in Publication Data
A catalogue record for this book is available from the British Library.

Library of Congress Cataloging-in-Publication Data
A catalog record for this book has been requested.

ISBN 978-1-4473-4807-8 (hardback)
ISBN 978-1-4473-4809-2 (ePub)
ISBN 978-1-4473-4810-8 (Mobi)
ISBN 978-1-4473-4808-5 (ePDF)

The right of Kharisma Nugroho, Fred Carden and Hans Antlov to be identified as authors of this work has been asserted by them in accordance with the Copyright, Designs and Patents Act 1988.

All rights reserved: no part of this publication may be reproduced, stored in a retrieval system, or transmitted in any form or by any means, electronic, mechanical, photocopying, recording, or otherwise without the prior permission of Policy Press.

The statements and opinions contained within this publication are solely those of the authors and not of the University of Bristol or Policy Press. The University of Bristol and Policy Press disclaim responsibility for any injury to persons or property resulting from any material published in this publication.

Policy Press works to counter discrimination on grounds of gender, race, disability, age and sexuality.

Cover design by Policy Press
Front cover: image kindly supplied by Mr. Armin Hari
Printed and bound in Great Britain by CPI Group (UK) Ltd,
Croydon, CR0 4YY
Policy Press uses environmentally responsible print partners

Contents

Acronyms		v
Foreword by Leonard VH Tampubolon		vii
Preface		xi
one	**Introduction: local knowledge matters!**	**1**
	Knowledge in policy processes	6
	Types of knowledge in policy processes	11
	Knowledge hierarchies	14
	The knowledge sector in Indonesia	20
	Local knowledge in policy making in Indonesia	22
	Outline of the book	24
two	**Forms of knowledge and policy influence**	**29**
	Types of knowledge in public policy making	30
	A typology of knowledge	32
	The interaction between knowledge sources: local knowledge and citizen participation	39
	Knowledge-to-policy processes and local knowledge	40
	Conclusions	42
three	**Local knowledge in democratic policy making**	**43**
	The study of meaning and local knowledge	44
	Public decision making, bureaucratic power and local knowledge	46
	Working politically	48
	Local knowledge and participatory development	53
	Conclusion	57

LOCAL KNOWLEDGE MATTERS

four	**Stories of local knowledge**	**59**
	Case study 1: Water for all – *Perkumpulan Pikul* (Pikul Association)	60
	Case study 2: 'Baleo! Baleo! Baleo!' – Poros Photo	63
	Case study 3: *Pranata Mangsa:* When traditional knowledge meets science – Centre for Anthropological Studies, University of Indonesia (PUSKA UI)	65
	Case study 4: Fish sovereignty in *sasi lompa*, Haruku – Centre for Regional Studies and Information (PATTIRO), Jakarta	69
	Case study 5: The river that brings life to the city – Institute for Islamic and Society Studies (LK3), Banjarmasin, South Kalimantan	73
	Case study 6: Wisdom fends off disaster in Pakis village – Bandung Institute for Governance Studies (BIGS)	75
	Case study 7: Revitalising *Keujruen Blang* – Centre for Education and Community Studies (PKPM), Aceh	78
	Case study 8: Blessings from *mawah* – Foundation for People's Welfare (YKU), Aceh Besar	81
	Case study 9: Zero compromise in Torong Besi – Centre for Politics and Government, Gadjah Mada University (POLGOV UGM)	83
	Case study 10: Traditional insurance – *Lembaga Advokasi HIV/AIDS (LAHA)* Institute for HIV/AIDS Advocacy, Kendari	85
five	**Generating and managing local knowledge**	**89**
	Generating local knowledge	89
	Interaction and adaption with the local environment	92
	Interaction between forms of knowledge	95
	Locality and origin	98
	The political economy of generating and managing local knowledge	103
	Methods and instruments to codify information and knowledge	106
	Methods and instruments to manage information and knowledge	111
	Conclusions	116
six	**Using local knowledge in policy making**	**119**
	How is local knowledge communicated?	119
	Who to influence	127
	The politics of local knowledge to policy	130
seven	**Conclusion: improving public policy through local assets**	**139**
	Knowledge assets and strategies	142
	New roles, new rules	146
	Going forward: a level playing field	147
References		**153**
Index		**167**

Acronyms

AMAN	Indigenous People's Alliance
Bappeda	Regional Development Planning Agency
Bappenas	National Development Planning Agency
BIGS	Bandung Institute of Governance Studies
BPJS Kesehatan	Social Security Implementing Agency for Health
CSO	Civil Society Organisation
DPRD	Regional House of Representatives
DPRK	Regional House of Representatives in Aceh
FAO	Food and Agriculture Organization
JATAM	Mining Advocacy Network
KSI	Knowledge Sector Initiative
LAHA	Institute for HIV/AIDS Advocacy, Kendari
LK3	Institute for Islamic and Society Studies, Banjarmasin
MAA	Indigenous Community Council, Aceh
Musrenbang	Development Planning Forum
NGO	Non-governmental Organisation
P3A	Community-based Water Management
PAMSIMAS	Community-based Drinking Water and Sanitation Provision Programme
PATTIRO	Centre for Regional Studies and Information, Jakarta

PKPM	Centre for Education and Community Studies, Aceh
POLGOV UGM	Research Centre for Politics and Government, Gadjah Mada University
PUSKA UI	Centre for Anthropological Study, University of Indonesia
Rp	Indonesian Rupiah (1 USD = 13,000 Rp)
UGM	University of Gadjah Mada, Yogyakarta
UI	University of Indonesia, Jakarta
WALHI	Indonesian Forum for Environment
YKU	Foundation for People's Welfare, Aceh

Foreword

Dr Leonard VH Tampubolon
Deputy Minister for Economic Affairs,
National Development Planning Agency (Bappenas), Indonesia

Indonesia is a plural nation-state made up of communities with diverse social backgrounds: ethnicity; customs; culture; language; and religion. Pluralism is the very fabric of the daily life of every Indonesian, and it is the basic capital for Indonesia to grow and develop into a strong nation. All elements of Indonesia's plural society need to work together to build harmonious social relations, strengthen cohesion and give priority to equality – not exploit differences – in order to realise the national motto, *Bhinneka Tunggal Ika* (Unity in Diversity).

The breadth and depth of knowledge and aspiration that emerges from local communities in Indonesia should become the basis for development policy formulation and implementation in this plural nation. Nevertheless, this has not always encouraged policy makers to a better understanding of the importance of knowledge about the local context for the planning cycle. References to policy implementation are mostly from empirical studies that often lack local context and relevance to the policy being discussed.

The mid-term evaluation of the Indonesian National Medium-Term Development Plan (RPJMN) 2015-2019 conducted by Bappenas in 2017 shows that two key issues that hinder the achievement of economic growth targets are low absorption of government spending and slowing private sector activity; these two are related to the structural barriers of policy implementation in technical and sub-national agencies. The results imply that despite implementation failure being the main problem, knowledge about implementation is still missing and needs to be further explored. The empirical experience in implementing government flagship programmes points to the importance of taking local context into account for the success of development initiatives.

Bappenas welcomes the publication of this book because it is relevant to addressing the increasingly complex development challenges we face in Indonesia, and to building our understanding of the role of local knowledge in the critical stages of the development cycle, especially in policy formulation and implementation. This book also represents collaboration between local communities as knowledge producers, local civil society organisations as managers and crafters of knowledge and district governments as the implementers of public policies at the sub-national level. In a joint effort to strengthen knowledge-based policy processes in Indonesia, this book is a product of a partnership between the Indonesian Government and the Australian Government, which are represented by Bappenas and the Australian Department of Foreign Affairs and Trade (DFAT).

The main contribution of this book is the presentation and processing of ten case studies on the link between practical discourse and social policy; on how local knowledge is produced, communicated and used to influence the overall policy cycle. Coupled with references to the rich literature on the topic, the authors invite us to reflect on the kinds of knowledge we often use to assess the reliability of knowledge in the policy-making process. Through presentations of empirical evidence in the policy cycle in the real world, the case studies demonstrate the knowledge-to-policy process at the local level, who is involved and how local knowledge can be effective in influencing public policy-making processes.

The main hypothesis of this book is that development policies will be more effective when using a variety of sources and types of knowledge, whether generated from academics, professionals or communities. Local knowledge is a valuable asset that contributes to national development, emphasising the close and interconnected relationship between culture and development. Development policies will be easier to implement if the local context and local knowledge are taken into consideration, because local knowledge anticipates technical feasibility, political dynamics and the socio-cultural dimension at the local level. This principle is important and highly relevant to the diverse development context in Indonesia. Bappenas hopes that this book will contribute to promoting the use of local knowledge in policy making in Indonesia.

Preface

In late 2014, KSI, the Knowledge Sector Initiative (Indonesia) hosted a research competition inviting proposals to look at cases where local knowledge had been used to influence public policy. There was an overwhelming response to the call with over 500 proposals submitted. We realised that we had hit on an untapped and under-researched area in the knowledge to policy process. We had funds for only ten projects so we chose those carefully from among the very best. They cover a wide range of subject areas and a broad range of cultural groups, political economies, and geographic regions within Indonesia.

In a one-day conference in April 2016, the researchers presented their cases to a broad audience of policy makers, researchers and civil society organisations. They made a compelling case that knowledge does not only come from the scientific studies that are carried out, but that stories of local knowledge that are well documented and well communicated also produce data that policy makers can and indeed need to use for effective implementation of policies. This was acknowledged by the Minister of the Indonesian National Development Planning Agency (Bappenas), citing a positive example of the use of local knowledge in road construction in North Sulawesi. A senior bureaucrat at the conference challenged one of the research teams that they did not actually have any data to back up their findings. The team very persuasively made the case that photographs documenting local knowledge are indeed sources of knowledge: each photograph includes many data points that help us understand and communicate local knowledge in ways that can reach policy makers.

Other partners pointed towards their use of drama, songs and stories. We realised then that we had an unusual treasure: a set of cases about how local knowledge plays a role in policy processes and how it, with other forms of knowledge, can co-create policy advice. While many policy researchers and academicians note the importance of other forms of knowledge in policy processes, little has been written with actual case material, particularly in Indonesia. Hence this volume.

We are deeply indebted to the researchers and institutions who developed the cases and engaged in dialogue about them. We thank the teams from PIKUL in East Nusa Tenggara; Poros Photo, for its work in East Nusa Tenggara; PUSKA-UI, the Centre for the Study of Anthropology at the University of Indonesia, for their study in West Nusa Tenggara and West Java; PATTIRO, the Centre for Regional Studies and Information, in Central Maluku; LK3, the Institute for Islamic and Society Studies, in South Kalimantan; BIGS, the Bandung Institute for Governance Studies, for their work in Central Java; PKPM, Centre for Education and Community Studies, in Aceh; YKU, the Foundation for People's Welfare, in Aceh; POLGOV-UGM, the Research Centre for Politics and Government at the University of Gadjah Mada, for their work in East Nusa Tenggara; and LAHA, the Institute for HIV/AIDS Advocacy, working in Southeast Sulawesi.

We especially want to thank the communities and government agencies with whom our partners engaged to complete their studies on the efforts made by those communities and government agencies to influence public policy. The process of writing the book was greatly facilitated by the clarity and level of detail in the cases that allowed us to identify the issues we present in the chapters.

We are also indebted to the participants in the conference where the researchers presented their findings. It was their interest and their responses that triggered the idea that these cases warranted more analysis and a much wider audience. We hope that our book can trigger more funding and support for looking at how all forms of knowledge can co-create better policies in support of social development, and that public officials at the national and subnational level can better appreciate citizen-generated knowledge.

PREFACE

We would be remiss if we did not also express our sincere appreciation for support from Bappenas and the Department of Foreign Affairs and Trade (DFAT) of the Government of Australia, who together guided the KSI project and encouraged the idea of this grant scheme and this book. And of course, we thank RTI International, the implementers of the KSI project for their support in the endeavour. We are grateful to the three anonymous reviewers whose comments improved the manuscript in important ways. Last, but not least, we thank the editorial team at Policy Press for their encouragement and support. All remaining errors are our own.

KN, FC, HA
Bangkok, Ottawa, Jakarta
15 November 2017

ONE

Introduction: local knowledge matters!

'The problem of knowledge is that there are many more books on birds written by ornithologists than books on birds written by birds or books on ornithologists written by birds.' (Naseem Nicholas Taleb, 2010: 77)

Indonesia, a diverse archipelago of 17,000 islands and more than 300 ethno-linguistic groups, has many rich sources of knowledge that are produced and communicated outside of formal research institutions. Local knowledge enriches policy making by providing context and improving targeting. Local knowledge channels new forms of knowledge to local policy makers. It can also revitalise traditional cultures and their expressions. However, it is easy to believe that scholarly research is more important for influencing public policy. We will suggest in this book that it is a mistake to ignore local knowledge, as it plays a key role in improving public policy at both local and national levels. Without local knowledge, science can find it difficult to influence policy. There is extensive disagreement about classifications of different types of knowledge (Agrawal, 1995; Briggs, 2005). We review and take a position on classification that focuses squarely on bringing local knowledge to the fore in policy processes. This volume seeks to identify how local knowledge has been developed and used in policy processes in Indonesia, and to situate local knowledge with other forms of knowledge that influence public policy. Our hypothesis is that the use of evidence in the public policy process will be more effective if all parts of the knowledge sector are actively engaged, and that building the functions of the knowledge sector and progressively linking them will enhance the use of high quality evidence produced and communicated by researchers, and used by policy makers. A sustainable knowledge sector[1] is based on research that is of high quality, is locally contextualised, and that can be used effectively in the public policy-making process. Developing policy responses to the complex social and economic challenges that Indonesia faces means that government agencies require access to increasingly sophisticated data and nuanced analysis from multiple sources to inform policy decisions. Democratisation is increasing demand from civil society for greater openness in the policy-making process, and decentralisation is providing local governments with the space to experiment with policy solutions relevant to local contexts and needs. This presents an important opportunity to integrate local knowledge in policy processes.

This volume represents an attempt to document the use of local knowledge in policy processes in Indonesia and as such we hope that it will be useful to practitioners seeking to understand and integrate local knowledge into their efforts to influence policy. In 2014, the Jakarta-based Knowledge Sector Initiative (KSI)[2] began exploring

---

[1] Which has usefully been defined as 'the institutional landscape of government, private sector, and civil society organisations that provide research and analysis to the development of public policy' (AUSAID, 2012, p iii).

[2] The Knowledge Sector Initiative (KSI) www.ksi-indonesia.org/en/home is a joint programme between the governments of Indonesia and Australia and works to improve the lives of the Indonesian people through high-quality public policies grounded in rigorous research, analysis and evidence. The KSI approach is system-wide and builds the knowledge-to-policy process by strengthening the delivery of high quality, policy-relevant research, the demand for evidence by policy makers, the ability to communicate evidence

local knowledge and how alternative forms of knowledge could influence and enrich public policy. We define 'local knowledge' as the knowledge that people in given communities or organisations have accumulated over time through direct experience and interaction with society and the environment. Local knowledge often deals with the same subject matter as scholarly research. However, local knowledge embodies different perspectives, meanings and understandings that are informed by local contexts and shaped by human interaction with the physical environment.

A competitive research grant scheme was announced in late 2014. The aim was to understand the role of local organisations in the production of local knowledge, channelling alternative knowledge to local policy makers, the mechanisms they use and the constraints and opportunities they face. The aim was to capture and promote innovation in knowledge-to-policy processes to encourage a broad range of players, a diversity of ideas, and novel means of communicating information to policy makers. Innovation was also expected in the creation of space for dialogue between coalitions of unlikely actors, on strategic public policy issues. The grant scheme targeted Indonesian civil society and community-based organisations, policy research institutes, and university-based research centres with direct experience in the use of local knowledge in public policy processes.

This current book is based on ten case studies selected competitively through this scheme from a pool of more than 500 proposals. The overwhelming response indicates the interest and demand for support for research on local knowledge. These cases were presented at a conference in Jakarta in April 2016, and subsequently turned into this book by the authors, who all worked at KSI at the time.

The ten case studies (presented in more detail in Chapters Four to Six) are listed in Table 1.1.

---

effectively to the policy process, and highlighting the critical barriers to the effective use of evidence in an enabling environment. All three authors worked for KSI at the time the Local Knowledge Scheme was launched.

LOCAL KNOWLEDGE MATTERS

Table 1.1 The ten case studies

Organisation/ Location	Purpose of Activity	Activity Description
Pikul Timor, East Nusa Tenggara	To explore ways to successfully manage community-based water management	The activity constitutes participatory research and documentation to study the management of community-based water resources on the island of Timor that are able to sustain both traditional and modern approaches. It maps the prerequisites of the successful management of water resources by the community, demonstrating success in resource management.
Poros Photo Lembata, East Nusa Tenggara	To conduct a visual ethnographic study to improve the welfare of traditional fishermen in East Nusa Tenggara	The activity aims to identify, document and systematise the coverage of village-based local wisdom among whale fishing communities on the island of Lembata, East Nusa Tenggara, and how they link to social policies and local government programmes.
PUSKA UI (Centre for Anthropological Studies, University of Indonesia) Indramayu, West Java and East Lombok, West Nusa Tenggara	To improve farmers' traditional and more recent empirical knowledge to respond better to climate change	This activity aims to advocate to policy makers that, in the midst of on-going climate change, it is important to combine farmers' traditional knowledge with agro-meteorological learning. The study also documents how scientific and local knowledge complement each other.
PATTIRO (Centre for Regional Studies and Information) Haruku, Central Maluku	To promote the contribution of local knowledge to maritime resources policy	This activity documents the traditional *sasi* local practice of resource sharing in maritime resources management in Central Maluku. *Sasi* is the hereditary local knowledge of indigenous people on the islands of Maluku that utilises natural resources and maintains environmental sustainability.
LK3 (Institute for Islamic and Society Studies) Banjarmasin, South Kalimantan	To revitalise river conservation culture to adapt to climate change through policy advocacy and urban development	The activity aims to encourage and support the government of Banjarmasin in South Kalimantan to consider preserving rivers and the culture of rivers through river revitalisation policies, to support and increase community participation in the revitalisation of the culture of the river. The study also documents links between religious and traditional knowledge.

INTRODUCTION: LOCAL KNOWLEDGE MATTERS!

Organisation/ Location	Purpose of Activity	Activity Description
BIGS (Bandung Institute for Governance Studies) Kendal, Central Java	To promote local knowledge relevant for the conservation of the Pakis Mountain Forest in Kendal, Central Java	This activity aims to understand the role of local knowledge used in community-based forest conservation among the people living in mountainous forests, and to build community forest conservation based on local knowledge.
PKPM (Centre for Education and Community Studies) Aceh Besar, Aceh	To revitalise local values and the role of *Keujruen Blang*, traditional institutions in Aceh Besar	The activity aims to identify local values in the community of farmers in Aceh Besar through a study of the existence, role and function of customary actors and institutions of *Keujruen Blang*, a traditional resource-sharing mechanism.
YKU (Foundation for People's Welfare) Aceh Besar, Aceh	To conduct a study on the role of the traditional *mawah* financial mechanism in supporting the livelihoods of vulnerable communities in Aceh Besar	The activity aims to identify and analyse the comparative advantages of a traditional profit-sharing system (*mawah*) and how it can collaborate with other existing formal and informal financial services in rural communities of Aceh Besar.
POLGOV UGM (Research Centre for Politics and Government, University of Gadjah Mada, Yogyakarta) Belu and Manggarai, East Nusa Tenggara	To strengthen local knowledge for natural resource management using case studies of farmers' resistance to mining	This activity aims to bridge, encourage and empower local knowledge that is used to influence policy making in extractive resource management. The activity facilitates and documents several local mechanisms employed and preserved by the community in producing knowledge related to resource management.
LAHA (Institute for HIV/AIDS Advocacy) South Konawe, Southeast Sulawesi	To develop a community-based insurance model using local knowledge from Southeast Sulawesi	The activity aims to assist the community to finance community healthcare through a traditional insurance system inspired by local values in South Konawe, Southeast Sulawesi. The long-term plan is to establish a community-based Health Insurance Management Agency.

This book is based on the personal experiences and expertise of the authors, combined with knowledge gained through the ten case studies. The cases are diverse: they are from Aceh, Java, Southeast Sulawesi, West Nusa Tenggara, East Nusa Tenggara, Kalimantan and Maluku (see Map 1.1 on page 7). They address forest management, water resources, maritime resource management, financial services, resistance to mining and other community topics. The cases represent influence in many domains. We will learn about the impact of documenting traditional forest management practices on reducing erosion, efforts to revitalise the traditional river culture, and the importance of poetry and songs in educating people on conservation and preservation.

Knowledge in policy processes

We start with a few words about what we mean by policy processes and evidence-based policy making, situating this conversation in the broader knowledge-to-policy debate (Pawson, 2006; Carden, 2009; Cartwright and Hardie, 2012). The most common depiction of this knowledge-to-policy process is as a cycle (see Figure 1.1) in which policy makers seek evidence; intermediaries – policy analysts, policy research institutes – interpret the question to researchers; if new research is needed, researchers set about producing it, otherwise they provide the intermediaries with the evidence; and the intermediaries in turn interpret it back to policy makers in ways that they can use for their specific purposes. Sometimes the connection is directly between a researcher and a policy maker, but the more common model uses intermediaries, reflecting some inability among researchers to communicate effectively with policy makers.

In reality, however, the process is not simple, nor a neat cycle. Many political, social and economic factors come into play, and there is seldom pure and direct influence of knowledge on policy. Figure 1.1 assumes that requests originate from policy makers, while researchers fulfil the requests and people with communication skills make sure that the policy makers understand so they can use the evidence. It is a model that largely ignores externalities: does the evidence interfere

INTRODUCTION: LOCAL KNOWLEDGE MATTERS!

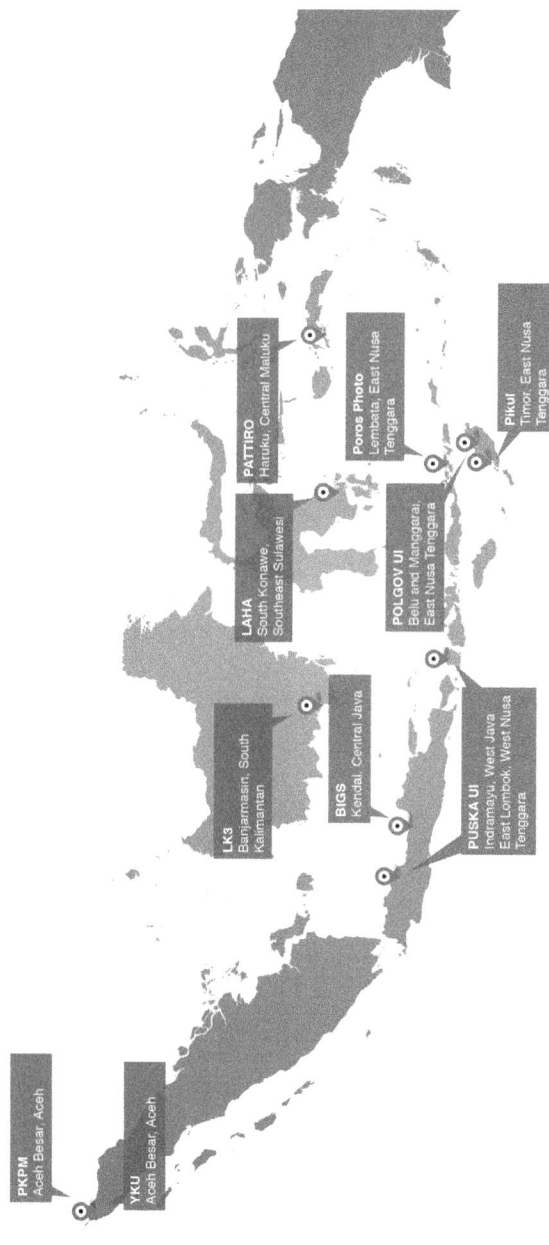

Map 1.1 Case study locations

Figure 1.1: A simple knowledge-to-policy cycle

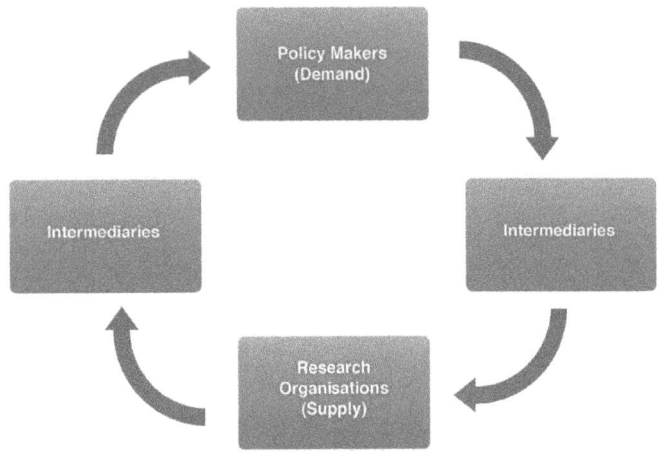

with the power of the policy maker? Does it fit the values of the political party in power? Research shows that often an issue is raised through research first and then brought to the policy process, so we need to allow for a range of starting points when considering the influence of evidence on policy processes (Carden, 2009). Further, this simple model assumes a clean and simple set of relationships, when in fact there are often many actors who play a role both directly and indirectly. Intermediaries who interpret may also have evidence to present themselves; local communities have knowledge, as do bureaucrats, religious leaders and others.

While this set of complications is increasingly recognised, there is still the tendency to accept the fundamental assumption that the knowledge that influences public policy is scientific knowledge. We set out to demonstrate that this is a narrow view that ignores the realities of knowledge generation and use. Without this broader view of knowledge, scientific knowledge can fall on deaf ears. The policy process is not the neat, clean process illustrated above. Rather, it is more like the messy image shown in Figure 1.2, in which multiple actors

INTRODUCTION: LOCAL KNOWLEDGE MATTERS!

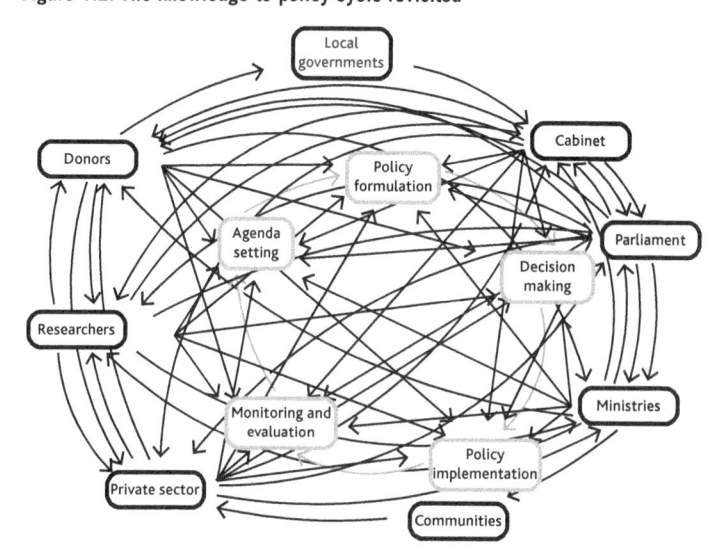

Figure 1.2: The knowledge-to-policy cycle revisited

Used with permission from the Overseas Development Institute (ODI).

with multiple value propositions and different bases of knowledge all interact in processes that ultimately lead to policy formulation.

This means that the role of evidence and knowledge is not just (or mainly) a technical process. In a technical process, such as building a bridge, knowledge about the construction and safety of the bridge affects the design and construction processes directly. Knowledge applied to policy processes is quite different. Instead of standing on its own merits, it must interact and compete with political values and cultural beliefs. As Parkhurst (2017: 66) notes, 'seeing policy making as defined by competition over interests and beliefs, and conceptualising the policy process as the arena through which that competition occurs, has fundamental implications for our understanding of the politics of evidence'. He goes on to make the point that we 'should expect to see strategic use of evidence by interest groups pursuing policy positions rather than seeing it as an aberration or somehow surprising' (Parkhurst, 2017: 67). Knowledge is used (often selectively) to advocate positions and argue a point of view. The former head of Australia's best-known government think tank calls this process 'a maelstrom of political energy, vested interests and lobbying' (Banks, 2009: 9). Carol Weiss referred to this as the 'percolation' of evidence (Weiss, 1979). As we will argue in Chapter Three, policy influence is strengthened when scientific, professional and local knowledge work together, co-producing influence.

Policy making is inextricably linked to policy implementation. In a wide-ranging review of policy implementation literature, Najam (1995) makes the point that policies are made where power resides (which could be at national, provincial or local level). And these policies are often implemented at other levels, in differing contexts and conditions. So, policy implementation is about managing the tensions between legally mandated instruments and resources and the environments in which the people meant to benefit from the policy live. Policy formulation at the highest levels of decision making, and policy implementation at street level, are not always synchronous.

This already challenging situation is further complicated when policies are nothing more than isomorphic mimicry, a common operating style to maintain the status quo. Isomorphic mimicry is defined by Pritchett, Woolcock and Andrews (Pritchett et al, 2010; Andrews et al, 2012) as a process whereby policy reform is limited to form and does not touch function. That is, no actual change takes place in how things are done, even though new policies are put in place in response to external pressure. Policies, whether based on some form of knowledge or beliefs and values, are not implemented and ultimately waste the resources of the state (while protecting the interests of some) and play against effective social and economic development.

A good example of challenges with knowledge – and the dangers of imposing a dominant understanding of local experience – is the recent book, *Papua versus Papua* (Suryawan, 2017), published in Indonesia about Indonesia's eastern-most province. The argument of the author is that there are *two* 'Papuas': one mainstream, as portrayed in academic literature (initially foreign but more recently also Indonesian), the other one as experienced, lived and defined by people in Papua. The author argues that the academic image of Papua has for decades been flavoured by ethnocentrism, orientalism and, in the end, imperialism. The reason the 'Papua question' is still unresolved after more than 50 years is that the central government mainly refers to the mainstream and imperial image of Papua and does not understand what is going on in the field. It thus imposes a naïve view of modernising Papua that has no local currency or makes the wrong policy decisions.

This is part of a larger problem. In a powerful book about indigenous research, Tuhiwai Smith (1999) argues that ethnocentrism and romanticism are common in western studies of indigenous people, often leading to misrepresentation through orientalism (Said, 1978). Western culture becomes the norm through which other societies are interpreted. As we will discuss, this is one of the limitations of 'scientific' sources of knowledge, based as it is on (non-indigenous) positivism. What we argue here is that the beliefs and lived experiences of a community – local knowledge – need to complement and perhaps even be the starting point for research about local cultures and communities.

Types of knowledge in policy processes

Local knowledge is one of three major types of knowledge that influence public policy (Figure 1.3). As with many classifications in the social sciences, the borders between knowledge types are porous, and no one tends to hold exclusively one type of knowledge. The most well understood and most common is academic research and scientific knowledge. Although it is often implicit, academic research is 'loaded with cultural, racialized, gendered, political and class assumptions' (Holmes and Crossley, 2004: 208). Providing opportunities for other types of knowledge to inform policy is thus inherently democratising and implies the participation of a broader group of legitimate actors to generate information. Because they often use different means of communication than academic research, other forms of knowledge can capture different meanings (Holmes and Crossley, 2004; Bryant, 2002). While this is generally an advantage, it also presents challenges in terms of communicating with policy makers. Officials may prefer modes of communication associated with academic research as legitimate for informing decisions. Further, groups providing local or professional knowledge may have different standing in policy makers' eyes, given their political identities and positions in the local social context, to the perspective on 'objective' information provided by researchers (Bryant, 2002). It will therefore be important to understand how officials receive other sources of knowledge, and how they choose to use them. Chapter Two presents a closer investigation of the types of knowledge indicated in Figure 1.3, namely: scientific knowledge, professional knowledge and local knowledge.

Figure 1.3: Types of knowledge and the policy influence space

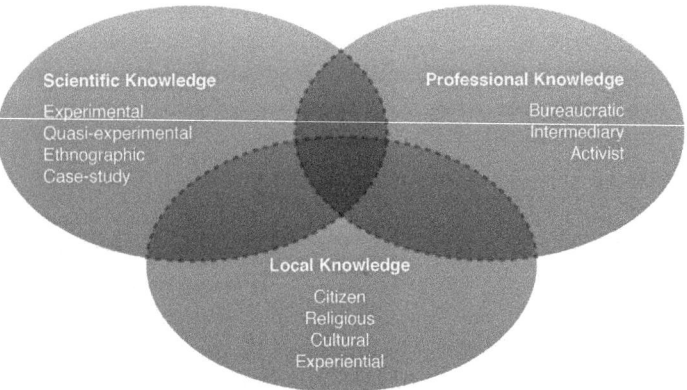

Throughout this book, the typology refers to the different sources and methods of knowledge generation while acknowledging some overlapping boundaries among them. This conception is distinguished from other categorisations of knowledge/evidence that are based on their utility, for example, evidence-based management, which is focused more on the different types of evidence used in decision making processes (Briner et al, 2009: 22) or Parkhurst's concept of the elements of the good governance of evidence (Parkhurst, 2017: 123).

The strength of understanding and using multiple forms of evidence is in how it can help navigate treacherous political economy terrain. As Najam argues, because there are multiple actors operating at different levels of the systems and in different contexts, 'actors must be the unit of analysis' (Najam, 1995: 32) for understanding policy making and its implementation. Our book explores the role of local knowledge in that process and makes the case that local knowledge is a powerful tool in improving policies and their implementation, as it brings more actors into policy-making processes. We fully recognise the point that Parkhurst (2017) makes: which evidence ultimately gets promoted is a political choice. We argue, though, that political choices are mutable and can be affected by actors within the system if they are aware of the political nature of a decision and can identify ways and means of bringing other forms of knowledge to the table. This book attempts to build an understanding of how that takes place through an analysis of cases from across the archipelago, highlighting the importance and potential of local knowledge, something that is often mentioned in the policy literature (for example, Jasanoff, 1990) but is seldom explored in depth. Much of the international literature reflects the view in Hernandez (2012: 153) that, 'there is little to no evidence that indigenous knowledge systems have received meaningful inclusion in public policy development'. At the same time, there is growing recognition of the potential of local knowledge to contribute, and efforts are underway to figure out how (FAO, 2004; Nordic Council of Ministers, 2015; Thaman et al, 2013; ICRAF, 2014; Simpson et al, 2015).

As generated through iteration and adaptation in day-to-day practices, local knowledge is highly relevant for a community's life. However, due to its locally specific context, it is inherently challenging for local knowledge to inform public policy, as public policy's coverage addresses the general population, and seldom addresses a specific context. Local knowledge, like other forms of knowledge, is most effective when multiple forms of knowledge interact to influence policy. Citizens seldom act based on one type of knowledge. Rather, their lived experience incorporates (to a greater or lesser degree) local, professional and scientific knowledge. While we as academics and scientists fully agree with the panel of eminent social scientists who put forward the case for the importance of science, and particularly social science, and for promoting its better use in public policy (National Research Council, 2012), we do not believe that this can be accomplished without a better understanding of other ways of knowing and other forms of knowledge that influence policy and policy makers.

Knowledge hierarchies

Knowledge evolves in a pervasive landscape of hierarchies that in different ways shape the journey to policy influence (Figure 1.4). First are the perceived unequal forms and domains of knowledge where scientific knowledge (often thought of as the natural sciences) traditionally occupies the leading position; the less 'exact' forms of knowledge (professional and local) are relegated to lower levels of prestige (Weiler, 2009).

The second hierarchy is in the realm of institutional arrangements for the production of knowledge. The credibility of knowledge is sometimes organised in terms of prestige, resources and influence of the institutions that generate the knowledge, and where they are located (in the global north or the global south), rather than by the quality of the knowledge itself. Under this same category falls the hierarchy within knowledge-related institutions, between professor and student, between institute directors and staff, between senior and junior faculty and, more subtly, between administrators and faculty.

The third hierarchy is in research methodology. Knowledge that is generated through a 'gold standard' methodology (randomised control trials, experimental research) is considered the top of the knowledge hierarchy. This view is strongly held in many quarters, but we dispute this type of classification of research methodologies and rather take the position that the best method is the one that is most suitable to the research question at hand. A report from the International

Development Research Centre (IDRC) argues that research quality cannot be divorced from its social relevance (Ofir et al, 2016: 4). Even scientific information is likely to be disregarded if it is seen as irrelevant to the needs of particular decision makers. In this process, taking socially relevant knowledge into account in social research will improve scientific relevance, legitimacy and stature.

The fourth is a hierarchy of knowledge based on the forms of its manifestation. In a world where science, civilisation, intelligence, wisdom and education are measured in terms of functional literacy and written documents, such as the number of books published and publication in peer-reviewed journals, local knowledge and oral wisdom would be permanently on the bottom of the knowledge hierarchy. This presents a challenge for an oral knowledge-based society like Indonesia. Ariel Heryanto (2015) argues that Indonesia would be a permanently sad story of the progress of civilisation or quality of education if the measurements were exclusively in terms of scholarly performance[3] or number of academic publications (Nugroho et al, 2016).

While the production of local knowledge is unstoppable because it is how a community makes sense of life, all of these hierarchies and relationships have been a disincentive for using local knowledge to influence policy. These hierarchies shape the basis for status and authority of local knowledge in the knowledge-to-policy realm; they have put the credibility of local knowledge in influencing policy at the lowest level. In this situation, local knowledge has little ability and credibility to legitimate power, so public policy makers have little interest in supporting a rise in the influence of local knowledge in policy making. This also means lower interest in investing resources for local knowledge development and application by policy makers. This might be understandable, as knowledge and power are connected by a relationship of reciprocal legitimation – that is, knowledge legitimates

---

[3] In 2015, Indonesia ranked 62 out of 72 countries in the Programme for International Student Assessment (PISA), a worldwide study of 15-year-old school pupils' scholastic performance on mathematics, science and reading.

Figure 1.4: Knowledge hierarchies and policy influence

Placement on hierarchy	Types of Knowledge	Institutional Arrangements of Knowledge	Methods in Knowledge Creation	Forms of Knowledge
High ←	Scientific	Prestige of Organisation	Experimental	Global Parchment
	Professional	Location of Organisation (North/South)	Quasi-Experimental	Publication
			Ethnographic	Literacy
Low	Local	Hierarchy within Organisation	Case Study	Oral Knowledge

power and, conversely, knowledge is legitimated by power (Flyvbjerg, 1991). This symbiotic relationship between knowledge and power has implications for the role of the university as the political partner of the policy maker. Because the university and other research institutions legitimise knowledge in the eyes of policy makers, local knowledge suffers multiple inequalities, which thwart its development. These inequalities are sustained by unequal relations with (and within) groups that hold economic, social, political, environmental and cultural power, and which impose an exclusive way of constructing local knowledge. Inequalities in knowledge also happen within a community whereby gender, age and ethnic origin affect the value assigned to knowledge.

Local knowledge is at play in many different arenas, so these hierarchies will help explain how it is an important part of the knowledge sector and how we can build it in more effectively in future. As Jones et al (2012) observe, local knowledge is usually tacit. Our volume represents an effort to make some of that knowledge, and how it has influenced public policy, explicit. The question is: whose knowledge matters? Whose knowledge is used in policy processes, and whose knowledge is not used, either because it is not considered knowledge or because it is thought to be less important? What these cases demonstrate is the diversity of influences on public policy. While much has been made of the role of scientific evidence, there is much less understanding of the role of other forms of evidence and knowledge in the public policy process, and limited recognition of the importance of the co-production of knowledge.

Armitage et al (2011: 996) described the co-production of knowledge as, 'the institutional trigger or mechanism that actually enables learning within co-management settings'. They are looking at the context of the Canadian Arctic, where science cannot address challenges without integrating local knowledge into their models. Simply put, co-production is the joint production of new knowledge by all those with some useful knowledge to contribute, be it science, technology, professional knowledge or local knowledge. Many other fields, for example a conference at the University of York on the implications in Web 2.0 (University of York, 2012); Sheila Jasanoff in policy research (Jasanoff, 2004); and applied health research (Heaton et al, 2016) recognise that in dealing with systemic and wicked problems, many players need to engage. The new knowledge that is needed to manage in these settings needs broad input, not only the input of 'experts'. There are many definitions of co-production but they all relate to the value of taking knowledge production out of the sole hands of scientists and integrating other knowledge that a society builds.

All forms of knowledge, including local knowledge, must be organised to be used in policy making. A diversity of knowledge sources is one hallmark of healthy policy making. Citizen-generated local knowledge is codified by community-based and civil society organisations, often through formal institutions of citizen participation, or through mass media (Jones et al, 2012). Citizen knowledge is generated in what is usually called civil society – the aggregate of non-governmental organisations (NGOs) and associational life that manifests the interests and will of citizens; it is at once a protector against the abuse of public or private power, a practical vehicle for the transformation of social values, and a space where alternative solutions to social problems can be developed and debated (Hall, 2003). A healthy, functioning civil society – and knowledge sector – builds relationships, cooperation and communication across sectors, borders and communities. NGOs can contribute to local knowledge by using a diversity of evidence, improving the quality of discourse, challenging capacity constraints, opening data for scrutiny and sharing knowledge with others (Hayman and Bartlett, 2013: 2).

Many studies show that evidence-based policy is still a big challenge, even in developed countries (Carden, 2009; Banks, 2009; Parthasarathy, 2011; Grant, 2014). Evidence-based policy making started to gain political currency under the Blair administration in the United Kingdom in the late 1990s, in a government with a reforming and modernising mandate, committed to putting an end to ideologically driven politics and replacing it with rational decision making. However, Rose (2017) in his article on Brexit, Trump and post-truth politics, reported that ideology and sentiment still have significant influence on policy making. Given the inherently political nature of policy making, strong evidence does not necessarily rank highest in the knowledge hierarchy. As we will see in Chapter Three, this has implications for how policy makers used different sources of knowledge, with a new form of 'populist' policy making emerging using more 'realist' (read, post-truth) evidence for policy proposals.

We started these local knowledge studies in 2014. Since that time, global changes have reinforced the importance of addressing local knowledge and ensuring the integration of local knowledge into decision-making processes. It is becoming more difficult to use evidence of any form in the face of these changes. Politics plays the leading role and political considerations are often more important than what evidence says. At its extreme, that has become 'post-truth politics' (Suiter, 2016). But this tendency has always existed: policy makers value political evidence more than other evidence. Appeals to emotion, ideology or dogma dominate, and factual rebuttal or fact checks are ignored on the basis that they are mere opinions. In 2016 there were two global instances where these types of citizens' opinions (mixed with politics) contradicted dominant bodies of knowledge: Brexit and the United States election. Both of these cases articulate a counter-culture as a reaction to the domination of traditional elites. Both had outcomes that surprised experts and the ruling elite. It must be noted that they are very different from the cases of local knowledge portrayed in this book – they are based on disenchantment, distrust and fear co-opted by populist politicians – but they provide an argument for diversifying our sources of knowledge. Mainstream politicians and media, not listening to this citizen-generated local knowledge, misread the 2016 public mood and thus allowed populist leaders to claim grassroots support. Learning from this, policy makers and experts must become better at capturing alternative world views.

We do not argue that we should disregard scientific evidence or expertise, quite the contrary. As policy development is unpredictable, there needs to be more data- and evidence-driven knowledge to inform the process, to make sure that decisions are taken on the basis of strong knowledge foundations. Nevertheless, local knowledge helps us with a framework to understand the different dimensions of the truth of the many.

In addition, previously closed planning and public policy making must be opened up and democratised. This is not about replacing scientific knowledge or experts (see Chapter Three). It is about enriching such knowledge by bringing in local sources and perspectives. Local knowledge has an important role to play in the creation of policy-relevant research and enriching the role of the expert. Policy making is not just about producing and using knowledge, it is also about promoting dialogue and building capacities. This has been described as a call for 'a new, plural, political ecology of knowledge' (Nandy, 1989: 267).

More than ever, we need to promote the use of evidence – all kinds of evidence – in anticipation of the failure of the post-truth approach to the world.

The knowledge sector in Indonesia

For a variety of reasons, Indonesia has not developed the kind of domestic knowledge infrastructure that is found in many developing countries (Guggenheim, 2012). Instead, the country has relied heavily on international technical assistance to help develop policy options that could be presented to high-level government decision makers – providing expert scientific knowledge. The main reason behind the lagging knowledge sector is the legacy of the authoritarian Suharto government (1966–1998) which ruled less by direct oppression than by using the machinery of the public administration to bring presumptively independent institutions (such as universities and think tanks) into its orbit and under the control of the bureaucratic state (Guggenheim, 2012: 48). This thwarted quality control and independent thinking and there was no incentive to base policy making on research and knowledge. It 'undermine[d] the production of knowledge from within the very institutions that created and used it' (Guggenheim, 2012: 142). A generation later, this legacy is still felt, with an entrenched public administration reluctant to give up its power. Although large state universities were provided with some autonomy in 2012, researchers at state universities remain constrained by a stifling civil service structure[4] and culture, and researchers at private universities and think tanks are constrained by inadequate funding. Although there have been improvements in the past few years, Indonesia's knowledge sector performs well below other countries of comparable economic standing in terms of university rankings, number of international publications, or patents (Guggenheim, 2012; Rakhmani and Siregar, 2016; Nugroho et al, 2016).

Notwithstanding, there are encouraging signs. A new generation of policy makers is coming to power, policy makers who were not trained under Indonesia's long authoritarian winter. Decentralisation is providing incentives for local leaders to be more sensitive to constituencies and local realities, and democracy has opened up for contestation and accountability (see Chapter Three). What is most important is that the complexity of being a middle-income country in an era of globalisation and in a sea of rapidly growing economies is finally catching up with top policy makers (including the popular President Joko Widodo elected in 2014) who are starting to see the importance of investing more in the knowledge economy and building a domestic and diverse knowledge sector. The Indonesian Academy of Sciences (*Akademi Ilmu Pengetahuan Indonesia* (AIPI)) is made up of leading scientists who provide important independent science policy advice to the nation. Until recently, AIPI was quite weak but is now beginning to strengthen its role as science advisor to the nation. An

---

[4] For example, the Indonesian civil service only allows staff to enter at a base level with minimal work experience. It does not allow for the recruitment of people from outside the civil service to middle and senior positions. A top university can thus only promote lecturers or professors from among existing civil servants, not look for the best candidates from private or foreign universities (see Nugroho et al, 2016). This promotes parochialism and weakens competition. However, a new 2014 Law on Civil Service is introducing competitive merit-based recruitment that, under certain conditions, allows for recruitment outside of the civil service. This will take time to have an impact on the system.

'Indonesian Science Agenda towards a Century of Independence' (AIPI, 2017) has been developed by AIPI's Young Academy and includes issues related to local knowledge.

Local knowledge in policy making in Indonesia

This mixed picture of the knowledge sector in Indonesia is significant for the knowledge-to-policy process. A recent study on the acquisition of knowledge by national decision makers in Indonesia (Datta et al, 2016) found that both the production of and demand for knowledge is weak. When decision makers used evidence, the main types of knowledge they considered were statistics, expert opinion and citizen perceptions (Datta et al, 2016: 6). Due to complex procurement rules, policy makers will seldom commission independent research. Instead, they read statistical reports, organise expert meetings or hold stakeholder workshops. What we call 'bureaucratic knowledge' in Indonesia is often the amalgamation of these reports, expert meetings and workshops.

Datta's study was of national policy makers and is an accurate reflection of policy making at the national level. However, as we will see in this book, experiments are happening and there are many innovations at the local level in which policies that are sensitive to local conditions are tested. Decentralisation of public policy-making processes has created opportunities for local knowledge to inform regional policy. The 'Big Bang' decentralisation, introduced in 2001, has given local governments more scope to interpret national policies, adapt them to the local context, and maximise their specific local needs and potential (Antlov and Hidayat, 2004). Competitive elections at national and sub-national levels, introduced in 2005, are seeing elected leaders being more accountable to citizens, while also providing opportunities for policy making based on better evidence and data from the field.

With decentralisation, greater decision-making authority and policy formulation rests with sub-national governments. Part of this decentralisation of policy making is the adoption of the Village Law

No. 6/2014. This law makes local communities part of development planning and budgeting processes. Under these circumstances, local knowledge can influence public policy-making processes in different ways. First, influence is generated through the 'pull factor', where demands from communities are presented for local context-specific policy; second, influence is generated through the 'push factor', the political process where local knowledge can be capitalised as electoral assets in the politics of representation. We discuss both later in this book.

Even though citizen perception was the third most common knowledge used by national policy makers, Datta's study found that when it actually was used, it was mainly to better understand a problem, not necessarily to improve implementation. In the next chapter, we discuss in more detail some of the challenges for the production and use of local knowledge. One issue in Indonesia is the historical disconnect between state bureaucrats as policy makers and the community and civil society organisations that generate and mediate local knowledge.

Indonesia has a rich history of knowledge produced outside of universities, going back to the nationalist movement of the early twentieth century, led by public intellectuals and opinion leaders who based their authority on a solid understanding of lived experience. A rich texture of social groups and movements has existed: religious societies, private schools, credit associations, mutual assistance self-help groups, neighbourhood organisations, water-user associations and many others (Ibrahim et al, 2007). As we will see in Chapter Four, there is a high level of citizen activism today in Indonesia – people doing budget analysis, public service oversight, community empowerment, legal aid and human rights advocacy. In this engagement, they generate knowledge that is locally relevant. There is enthusiasm and energy around finding local solutions to local problems, and in this process challenging the mainstream top-down development paradigm of prescribed technical solutions. There are thousands of citizen-based social action groups around Indonesia in which concerned citizens collaborate to solve local problems, and who share a desire to affect policy making and see public funds reallocated to benefit their constituencies (Antlov and Wetterberg, 2013: 200).

Local politics in Indonesia has been characterised as predatory interests nurtured under the Suharto regime's formerly vast, centralised system of patronage that has largely remained intact, even though with a new class of rent-seekers (Hadiz, 2003). Civil society activists in Indonesia have been characterised as 'floating democrats' hovering above, and not connected to, Indonesian society, and thus unable to gain popular legitimacy and muster a broad base sufficient to mobilise political support or influence (Manning and van Diermen, 2000; Priyono et al, 2007). The compromised democracy that emerges as a result does not empower ordinary people, as the spaces opened up through this form of democratic decentralisation are captured by various forms of 'predatory interests' (Hadiz, 2003) or 'bad guys' (Törnquist, 2002).

The political and economic decentralisation introduced in the early 2000s has contributed to the marginalisation of local community interest (Aspinall and Mietzner, 2010; Nasution, 2016). However, it has also created new opportunities for adoption of local knowledge in the public policy process. Decentralisation, according to Pisani, Kok and Nugroho (2017), has increased local policy makers' receptivity to local knowledge where local knowledge is presented as *aspirasi lokal* (local aspirations) and codified as an electoral asset. The present decentralisation process and the rise in political democracy in Indonesia also neglect local aspirations and knowledge. This is because the heads of the local governments and the members of local parliaments, who are supposed to be accountable to the community through regular elections, are mainly accountable to political parties and not the local community.

Outline of the book

This book will focus on the processes and mechanisms of how local knowledge:

- is produced;
- is communicated;
- interacts with other forms of knowledge;
- is received by policy makers and may be used to influence policy.

Chapter Two is about the various forms of knowledge described in Figure 1.3: scientific, professional and local knowledge, and how they interact. We will show that both scientific and professional knowledge are often privileged, simplifying and possibly undermining policy processes. Policy processes include multiple actors, operating at different levels of the system, in diverse contexts. Influencing that process means understanding the multiple knowledge bases that are at play among these actors and using them to identify and define policy options that will resonate with those who ultimately have to put them in place. The options may resonate for political reasons (such as public pressure), value-based reasons, or economic and social reasons. There is no one best reason and no one best approach. The best opportunity for success in influencing policy processes rests in understanding the many forms of knowledge that are at play and in being able to work with them, ideally in some form of co-production, to improve policies and their implementation. The policy process is enriched when multiple forms of knowledge are used; for local knowledge this presents an opportunity to expand its reach and relevance.

Chapter Three sets the frame for thinking about the cases of local knowledge use in Indonesia. It goes into more depth on the importance of local knowledge in democratic policy making. Building on the argument that local knowledge is political, we look at how this knowledge plays a key role not just in policy formulation but also in implementation. Local knowledge is generated by citizens in everyday conversations and forums, often articulated in civil society and popular participation. We argue for local knowledge as a prerequisite for the democratisation of policy making and the improvement of public policies. The new role of 'experts' is to support communities to understand policy options, and to provide a level playing field and opportunities for deliberative democracy more generally. Experts also help citizens understand and discuss the complex issues that affect their lives.

Chapter Four introduces the ten local case studies to give a sense of the richness of local experiences. The chapter focuses on approaches, achievements and challenges in supporting and understanding cases of local knowledge: how local knowledge is generated, managed and used in real time by local communities and NGOs.

The following two chapters will use these case studies to enrich the arguments presented in Chapters One to Three.

Chapter Five focuses on the generation and management of local knowledge. There are different positions and roles of organisations in producing local knowledge: to solve a problem, to recommend alternative ways to solve a problem, to anticipate potential problems and to preserve local wisdom. These different roles are defined by different capacities of organisations in understanding local issues and knowing the local political context, including its related stakeholders. All organisations believe that traditional wisdom and value located in the community must have a place and influence on local regulations, as they bring the voice of the people and communal strength to the table. Using data from the case studies, we demonstrate where local knowledge has been successfully presented to the local government resulting in policy recommendations; in some other cases, the work has only been able to function as awareness raising of local stakeholders. In a third category, some cases present local knowledge that is not yet linked to local policy but has been demonstrated as contributing to the quality of life of the community. Here, implementation precedes policy change, a fairly common occurrence when communities recognise the value of a change before the policy makers are ready to act.

Chapter Six focuses on the conditions under which local knowledge can influence policy. Some of our partners were successful in building communication with local policy makers and secured a position in the policy discourse. In general, we found that partners located where their projects were taking place were more able to advocate policy recommendations to local government. This appears to be because they have built relationships with local leaders and they have strong organisational reputations in the community. Some have been able to attract the attention of local leaders to their research results, which have then been implemented at a local level. It is critical to understand whether policy makers are able to draw meaning from and make use of the types of information generated by civil society organisations. Some mechanisms are identified which will help secure meetings with policy makers to present recommendations to them.

The conclusion in Chapter Seven puts the case studies in the context of different sources of knowledge. We present a number of tensions at play between local, professional and scientific knowledge. These tensions are the tapestry of building knowledge and a way to describe the fact that the pursuit of multiple and competing values, ends and benefits inevitably give rise to challenges about how to achieve balance. We also look at the implications of the new framework both for the academic study of various forms of knowledge, and for development practitioners working to improve or influence public policies.

TWO

Forms of knowledge and policy influence

This chapter argues that there are many types of knowledge that contribute to a society's body of knowledge. While the common perception of 'knowledge' is often limited to formal scientific knowledge, professional knowledge also matters, as does local knowledge. In professional knowledge, we include bureaucratic knowledge, without which many issues would not be able to make their way to policy makers. Those who work in policy research institutes and think tanks also produce professional knowledge: they can use and integrate evidence from scientific research with issues relevant to policy makers around local economy and politics in ways that make the evidence relevant, and, what is more important, usable by policy makers. This type of professional knowledge may be described as intermediary knowledge. Advocacy organisations, using activist knowledge, can use research evidence in similar ways to promote their agendas. Along with citizen evidence as part of local knowledge, religious knowledge can also play an important role. This chapter argues that if we ignore these forms of knowledge, if we treat them as irrelevant and assume that scientific evidence on its own can influence the policy process, we are missing some critical elements for success. Each plays an important role and brings different evidence to the policy maker. Without local interpretation and the intermediary, activist and bureaucratic knowledge that moves ideas to policy makers, we are unlikely to see much influence of scientific knowledge. Before we turn to a more detailed treatment of local and citizen-generated knowledge as the primary focus of this book, this chapter gives an overview of the different forms of knowledge and how they interact with each other in the policy-making process.

As we will see in the descriptions of types of knowledge and in their applications, the categories are porous. No one sits squarely within one type of knowledge; we all use multiple sources of evidence, but we do tend to have a preference and put one above the others in assessing a situation and making a decision. Co-production, which requires a respect for knowledge which we ourselves do not prioritise, is inherent in some senses, but there is a need to make it more explicit and reflect the relevance of all forms of knowledge in that process. Each type of knowledge manifests in several different ways, as we saw in Figure 1.3.

Types of knowledge in public policy making

There is growing consideration of different forms of knowledge in the policy space (Jasanoff, 2012). Knowledge is produced in many different places and in many different ways. We argue here that the public is not only a consumer of knowledge but also a producer. Even bureaucrats who are consumers of knowledge for the drafting of public policy recommendations are also producers of knowledge. All forms of knowledge should have a place in a flourishing knowledge sector.

The pre-eminence of scientific knowledge has overshadowed the roles of other forms of knowledge in most of the research on the role of evidence in public policy making. While there has been much written about the role of the citizen and problems with too much focus on experts (Easterly, 2015; Eyben et al, 2015), and there is a whole field of literature on the role of citizens in governance,[1] there has been much less consideration given to the roles of different forms of knowledge

[1] Including Goss, 2001; Fischer, 2003; Boyte, 2004; Gastil and Levine, 2005; and Chambers, 2012.

in policy making, as opposed to the identification of community needs. The citizen is not thought of as a holder of knowledge, as one who produces knowledge that could be useful to the policy process (an important exception to note here is Chambers, 2012). Rather, the citizen is treated as one who is affected by policy. The discussion has been largely about the need to ensure adequate and appropriate consultations with citizens. Citizens are expected to respond to scientific evidence or attempt to refute it with other scientific evidence and scientific knowledge. They are invited to participate, to present opinions and perspectives on the known scientific evidence, rather than to bring new and different knowledge to the process (Nadasdy, 2003). Where citizens come from a different cultural or knowledge base, such as indigenous communities, this adds to the challenge. With its more than 300 different cultural groups and more than 55 per cent of the population in two main ethnicities, Indonesia faces particular challenges in this regard. The argument is that the range of views needs to be heard, various perspectives considered and multiple values taken into account (see Chapter Three), but the common assumption is still that the evidence and knowledge to be considered is scientific. This is seldom questioned.

In the same way, bureaucrats are not thought of as producers of knowledge. Equally, consultants who consolidate the research of others in their representations are not thought of as knowledge producers but as consumers of scientific knowledge. Think tanks, or policy research institutes, form a bridge, as many are both producers and consumers of scientific knowledge. Citizens, bureaucrats and think tanks are expected to engage with the processes and systems that have been set up to consult on scientific evidence. For much local and traditional knowledge, this is a particularly difficult transition and the knowledge presented in scientific forums seems out of place and spurious. It is treated as views and opinions and sometimes as quaint. We need some new ways to think about the relationships between different types of knowledge and to build acceptance of different forms of knowledge in policy processes.

A typology of knowledge

Chapter One identified three main types of knowledge that influence policy (based on previous typologies such as that of Aristotle, as well as Hunt and Shackley, 1999). Aristotle defined three types of knowledge: *episteme, techne* and *phronesis*.[2] *Episteme* is about the explanation of phenomena, usually referred to now as science. *Techne* is about the technical knowledge we possess, or what we will call professional knowledge. And *phronesis* is about how we 'contribute to society's practical rationality in elucidating where we are, where we want to go, and what is desirable according to diverse sets of values and interests' (Flyvbjerg, 2001: 167). This is a type of citizen-generated local knowledge. The types of knowledge described here are not monolithic. Each is manifested in different ways and some illustrations are provided, such as bureaucratic knowledge as a form of professional knowledge, and religious knowledge as a form of local knowledge (Chapter Three). It should be clear that the categories are porous and most of us carry knowledge from different parts of this typology, but many of us privilege one form of knowledge over the others in our decisions. Like any typology it is a device to help us sort and identify patterns and ways of acting.

The first form is **formal scientific knowledge** that produces data sets from which we can extract conclusions about the state of the community and draw inferences about what that means for policy revision. Formal scientific knowledge gained stature in the (European) Age of Enlightenment, starting in the eighteenth century when ideas were presented based on logic and scientific reason, leading to the Scientific Revolution.[3] This movement led to an explosion of thinking and perspectives about evidence and reason. Formal scientific research has many tools on which to draw, whether for research on natural science issues such as climate change, or research on social

---

[2] As explained in Flyvbjerg (2001).

[3] Described by Thomas Kuhn (1962) in *The Structure of Scientific Revolutions* as a paradigm shift in how we think about science and evidence.

change that tries to understand what will influence new behaviours in a community to improve health and wellbeing. Academics will collect scientific evidence using qualitative and quantitative methods. This evidence will be contested by the academy and some of it will be presented to policy makers to inform their decisions. This formal scientific knowledge is the knowledge that has been the focus of much effort – to have policy makers consider it and use it in public policy. It is often the 'evidence' in evidence-based policy making.

In thinking about the influence of knowledge on public policy, we therefore tend to privilege the 'expert', the scientist who is presumed to have superior knowledge and superior evidence. A great deal of research and writing has been done on the use of scientific evidence in the policy process (Jasanoff, 1990; Kingdon, 1984; Carden, 2009). It is indeed important and many cases have been written and many frameworks presented on how influence happens.

The key actors in this group are research scientists. They are often in universities, but sometimes in research institutes (which may be publicly or privately funded). Solid scientific evidence, well presented, is important. The climate debate has seen the rise of evidence in the discussion, from the early days when research was preliminary and questioned, until now when the vast majority of people believe that the evidence is compelling and that something must be done. International agreements, national and even local legislation have been influenced by concerns about climate change. Science has played a very influential role here.

The second form of knowledge we call **professional knowledge** (Aristotle's *techne*, or what Hunt and Shackley refer to as *fiducial knowledge* and what Jones et al refer to as *practice-informed knowledge*).[4] Professional knowledge is produced as a service to policy makers. We identify three forms of professional knowledge: bureaucratic, intermediary and advocacy. All three reflect the ability of particular groups to relate knowledge to practice in ways that have the potential

---

[4] We prefer 'professional knowledge' as a term more easily communicated than 'fiducial knowledge'. It is broader than 'practice-informed knowledge'.

to influence; bureaucratic knowledge is most practised within the bureaucracy, intermediary knowledge is practised in think tanks, and advocacy knowledge is practised largely by advocacy groups. Professional knowledge is based on faith or trust that knowledge producers have made fair and honest use of the primary evidence and knowledge in their policy advice, that they have a good understanding of the context in which a decision has to be taken, and that they have not manipulated the evidence primarily for their own gain or purpose. It is for this reason that the reputation of a think tank is so important: it is taking primary research and often combining it with other knowledge that allows it to articulate the meaning of evidence for the policy maker. If its reputation suffers because of manipulation of evidence, or succumbing to a special interest group, its ability to influence is lost until it can rebuild its reputation. Professional knowledge is usually based on secondary sources of information as well as on the lived experience of its practitioners and their knowledge about the context and processes within which the knowledge is used. Whether bureaucratic, intermediary or advocacy knowledge, it synthesises and consolidates ideas and connects them to the context in which the policy operates.

Professional knowledge serves as a bridge between scientific knowledge and the needs of policy makers. It helps with the translation of scientific knowledge; its practitioners see themselves as capable of understanding both the scientist and the policy maker. They are usually not generating new basic knowledge; rather they are looking at research findings through a different lens and synthesising evidence that comes from different sources according to the needs of their clients and the contexts in which they are operating. Without professional knowledge, much scientific knowledge would not find its way into the policy space.

To be successful, producers of professional knowledge need to have both a strong understanding of research and a strong understanding of the needs of the policy makers who are their clients. Skills in knowledge translation and communication are central. Being able to interpret the evidence in ways that are meaningful to the policy community is not easy. It is one that few scientists master, therefore producers of professional knowledge play a key intermediary role, often defined as 'policy analysts' in a government employment structure.

Box 2.1 The art of the possible: bureaucratic knowledge as a form of professional knowledge

We present one form of professional knowledge which plays a major role in policy processes even though it is not often thought of as knowledge: bureaucratic knowledge. This is a form of knowledge in which bureaucrats are not only users but also producers of knowledge. As Zimmerman (n.d.) argues, bureaucracies are very good at codifying tacit knowledge into rules and regulations. Zimmerman further argues that other organisations can learn from and use the discipline of documenting knowledge that bureaucracies embody.

Bureaucracy translates and synthesises knowledge into frameworks that are relevant for a specific community of users. What a Ministry of Finance might need to know for a policy decision may be quite different from what a Ministry of Environment might need to know; and it might look at things through a very different lens. Bureaucratic knowledge guides the synthesis and framework development that will assist the different policy makers in their task. It reflects the ability of the bureaucrats to make sense of evidence in ways that respond to the specific needs of the policy makers with whom they are working. In that sense it is also knowledge generation, not only knowledge utilisation.

Bureaucratic knowledge is essentially knowledge about processes and contexts. These are important because they define what is possible in any policy context. Understanding the limitations and parameters of policy action is the knowledge that the bureaucracy brings. This is a crucial element in policy influence and is lacking in scientific and local knowledge. It is the bureaucrats in the positions of influence who most deeply understand the processes and the changing contexts within which a policy decision is made. Without that knowledge, influence is limited. This is more than simply about tactics. Like much professional knowledge, a lot of it is implicit, absorbed through years of observation and practice. It is made explicit through rules and systems, but these are particularly weak at capturing context due to its ever-changing nature, and they are quite limited in capturing process. Formal process steps are captured but the informal processes, the real power relations and issues, remain implicit.

What bureaucratic knowledge must do is simplify complex ideas and be selective about what can be done in each context. This requires a deep knowledge of the processes and contexts that are at play and a capacity to synthesise and translate knowledge into useful and useable evidence. It also requires an ability to keep the complexity of the issue in mind so that the simplifications are always well focused.

Bureaucratic knowledge is highly specialised. It builds synthesis from many kinds of evidence; it is created out of a deep understanding of practice in bureaucracy and an understanding of the operating context; it requires insider knowledge and strong understanding of the needs and expectations of decision makers. As a form of professional knowledge, bureaucratic knowledge makes significant contributions to policy processes. Without strong bureaucratic knowledge it can be a challenge to use scientific and local knowledge for policy influence. Bureaucratic knowledge is often the gatekeeper and should never be underestimated. However, at its worse (and this is often the case in Indonesia) 'bureaucratic knowledge' is nothing more than a collection of administrative reports, expert meetings and workshops.

The third type of knowledge, **local knowledge**, will only be discussed briefly here, as it is the subject of the rest of this book. Local knowledge emerges from a society's experience and practice. It is sometimes referred to as citizen knowledge (Jones et al, 2012), experiential knowledge or craft knowledge.[5] Durose and Richardson (2016) reference Henry Mintzberg who makes the point that policy must not rely on science alone but also on 'art', which includes among other things local knowledge. A great deal of the knowledge we hold as individuals is experiential knowledge. It is the knowledge we have about how to act in our communities, what values are important in the societies in which we live, and what will give us access or make us outcasts. We learn how to cross a street using experiential knowledge – we learn that hand gestures help us, or that in some places we must cross at traffic lights. The framework developed by the Food and

[5] Craft knowledge is often tacit, the knowledge we possess on how to complete a task. Often, it is not written down but passed down orally or by demonstration. See, for example, Wood (2006). Experiential knowledge is described as 'truth based on personal experience' (Borkman, 1976).

Agricultural Organization (FAO) (2004) is a useful starting point to navigate different forms of types of local knowledge:

- *Common knowledge* is held by most people in a community – almost everyone knows how to cook rice (or the local staple food).
- *Shared knowledge* is held by many, but not all, community members – villagers who raise livestock will know more about basic animal husbandry than those without livestock.
- *Specialised knowledge* is held by a few people who might have had special training or an apprenticeship – only a few villagers will become healers, midwives or blacksmiths.

Local knowledge is often implicit or tacitly held by citizens in a community. That is, we learn it by observing others or by trial and error. We seldom articulate it or create files about it. We learn it over time, through our actions and how others respond to us. Local knowledge helps us understand how to act in our homes, in our work places and with our friends. It helps us understand what is healthy and what is dangerous. It helps with practical matters in agriculture as well, as Grenier (1998: 50) notes from a study in Bali that, 'villager descriptive knowledge for trees, bamboo, and soil resources was, at the very least, equivalent to, and likely more detailed than, corresponding data from trained scientific researchers'. Local knowledge is generated by citizens from a broad range of different communities in everyday conversations and forums, often articulated in civil society and through popular participation. It is part of a contextual and living discourse, contested through everyday interactions and through interpretation by citizens of the multiple forms of knowledge that are part of their lived experience – the social capital that allows individuals to become citizens and establish communities.

A challenge to using local knowledge and sharing it with other communities, such as the policy community, is that it is often passed on through oral tradition and has not been codified. Codifying it becomes part of making it accessible for use and transmission to policy makers and other communities, as we will see in Chapter Five. Codifying local knowledge also risks bureaucratising it and freezing it in time.

Local knowledge is seen by those who hold it as co-production between communities and their environments.[6] As such, it is constantly evolving and changing, just as other forms of knowledge change with new learning and new situations. Local knowledge is also place-based and its ownership is diffused rather than centralised. It is the groups that use particular local knowledge that hold it (be they men, women, children, farmers, fishers, or any other group) and evolve it as part of both their survival and economic and social development. Our case studies used a range of definitions of local knowledge:

- a knowledge system – on farming and climate adaptation (PUSKA), against mining (POLGOV UGM), on forest conservation (BIGS) and on river-based living in South Kalimantan (LK3);
- local innovation – a community's local economy called *mawah* in Aceh (YKU), or a community health insurance system in Southeast Sulawesi (LAHA);
- indigenous practices – embodying traditional lifestyles relevant for the conservation and sustainable use of natural resources, for example, whale hunting in Lembata (Poros Photo), clan-based water management in Kupang (Pikul), *sasi* eco-friendly fishing in Maluku (PATTIRO) and community-based water management in Aceh Besar (PKPM).

Key actors in this space are advocacy organisations, community leaders, religious leaders and practitioners of traditional medicine. Here, too, there are overlaps with actors in the professional knowledge space. As we will see in Chapter Six, advocacy organisations can play a

[6] Co-evolution refers to the continuous and dynamic process of mutual adaptation between humankind and the natural environment. The co-evolution theory shows how social (for example, knowledge systems) and ecological systems are interconnected, and how they influence one another. Co-evolution leads to constant adaptations to changing environments, which in turn leads to increased diversity (Blaikie, 1992, as cited in FAO (n.d.)).

particularly important role because their success depends on a good understanding of the political space, but their origins are often in protecting communities on an issue that is deeply important to the leadership and is often embedded in local knowledge (an example would be the Indigenous People's Alliance (AMAN) in Indonesia).[7]

The interaction between knowledge sources: local knowledge and citizen participation

Policy influence is strengthened when scientific, professional and local knowledge work together. The ability to work across these different types of knowledge is the special skill of an informed and engaged citizenry. It is often manifested in the policy entrepreneur (Kingdon, 1984). A policy entrepreneur may come out of any form of knowledge but is someone who is capable of integrating the other forms of knowledge into their arguments and advocacy, and through that bring different sides together around a common agenda. They are leaders in processes of co-production of knowledge. The cases illustrate the importance of relationships (between types of knowledge and different communities in the policy process), communication (of ideas, values and beliefs), networking (to use other resources to understand the political process) and institutional change. While local knowledge is applied by the producers and social actors themselves in their daily lives, scientific knowledge (and to a lesser degree professional knowledge) is diffused by agents who do not put it into practice themselves (Olivier de Sardan, 2005: 159).

Consistent with the argument we make here, Durose and Richardson (2016) make the case for a co-production model of policy making, treating all forms of knowledge as part of the process. Quoting some of their colleagues, they suggest that 'co-production suggests the value of involving different forms of knowledge and expertise in the policy process, and even moves towards synthesis of different 'ingredients' of a policy puzzle', while ensuring that these different forms of knowledge

[7] See www.aman.or.id

are 'integrated, not annihilated, not absorbed' (Durose and Richardson, 2016: 40–41).

Each form of knowledge has several types of associated organisations. These categories are, however, porous and only represent where the predominant knowledge generated takes place in each organisation type. Universities provide professional knowledge in addition to their mandate around the accumulation of scientific knowledge, while policy research institutes may carry out research or be part of local knowledge in a particular field. Advocacy organisations may, and often do, operate with all types of knowledge. They are independent knowledge actors in the policy influence space, although they often act together with citizen groups and are often stronger when they do act together to bring several types of evidence to bear on a policy problem or on an effort to influence a policy maker.

Beyond normative democratic arguments, there are empirical reasons why it is useful to diversify sources of knowledge in policy making. As outlined in the Australian Government's *Women in Leadership Strategy* (DFAT, 2015), empirical evidence shows that diverse teams and sources of knowledge produce stronger outcomes. For example, research studies have demonstrated that organisations with a critical mass of women in senior management perform better across a range of performance markers than organisations with less gender diversity in senior management. 'The wisdom of crowds', as one influential book calls it, is superior to decisions taken by a few (Surowiecki, 2004). There is a simple business case for improving diversity and involving more people in decisions: it makes decisions better.

Knowledge-to-policy processes and local knowledge

As we saw in the Introduction, 'knowledge to policy' is the process through which data, evidence and other forms of knowledge are created, turned into policies and implemented in 'a maelstrom of political energy, vested interests and lobbying' (Banks, 2009: 9). It is to this maelstrom we now turn.

This process is not only about more sophisticated and accessible data, but a better understanding of the social context of knowledge and the relationship of social science to political deliberations. Policy making needs a wider range of contextually sensitive evidence and arguments brought to bear on a policy issue or social problem – investigating an increased number of relevant perspectives and adding more sources of knowledge. This is a refined understanding of the interactions that construct reality, the way that the empirical is embedded in the normative. If Stephen Lukes (1974) is correct that power shapes our preferences, we need to have a more astute understanding of the social and political context of policy making.

Local knowledge stands in concert with scientific or professional knowledge. Our case studies show the different ways that citizens can generate their own discourse that often acts as a counterpoint with the dominant development framework. This requires effort to strengthen local groups, allowing them to limit the indiscriminate extraction of local knowledge, to negotiate the way that research is carried out, to have a say in terms of intellectual property of local knowledge, and to defend local knowledge as their own treasure which belongs to their communities while not turning against 'the other'. In this situation, local knowledge needs a clearer definition and role as 'a common sense for people who share a communal sensibility' (Geertz, 1983).

As a taster of what will come, the BIGS case in this volume (case study 6, Chapter Four) looks at how local and professional knowledge had to come together in a process of co-production of knowledge to solve a challenge. It reminds us that the process can be long and detailed and that it sometimes requires institutional change. BIGS is codifying local knowledge on forest management on the densely populated island of Java. On Java, deforestation and the consequent erosion and loss of topsoil are leading to reduced productivity and severe flooding in many areas. While codifying local knowledge and practices that can mitigate deforestation, BIGS is beginning to bring local government officials into discussions and to see the practices in use. It is working towards integrating principles contained in local knowledge into policies for forest conservation.

Conclusions

So, whose knowledge matters in the policy process? We have made the argument that there are multiple forms of knowledge and they all play a role in public policy. We have further argued for the crucial role of citizen engagement and the importance for all to recognise the multiple forms of knowledge at play in any policy process. As a society, we have tended to privilege scientific knowledge but we have discussed examples of other forms of knowledge, and as the cases in this volume clearly illustrate, local knowledge matters and plays a role. Beyond individual forms of knowledge, interaction is often critical.

Professional knowledge is often the venue to translate scientific evidence and other types of knowledge into politically effective knowledge needed for policy making. Bureaucratic knowledge, for example, is a key feature of much policy influence. The bureaucrats know how the system works, they understand how to get ideas across to decision makers, and they can block ideas if they choose. Scientific knowledge producers must learn how to present their evidence in policy-relevant ways and must learn how to work with bureaucratic and other forms of professional knowledge to have an influence. Local knowledge does not always interact easily with bureaucracy, but in connection with other forms of professional knowledge it can play an important role. Sometimes the interaction is not through intermediaries but through an idea that directly captures the imagination of a policy maker.

Finally, we cannot ignore the fact that evidence and knowledge are not alone in influencing policy (Glover, 2015). Knowledge producers must present the best possible evidence and they must present it as persuasively as possible. But scientists and other knowledge producers must recognise that the evidence is not always paramount. Politics, beliefs and values play central roles and knowledge must dance with these influences to find its place.

THREE

Local knowledge in democratic policy making

As discussed in the Introduction, a diversity of knowledge sources is a hallmark of healthy policy making. But not all voices and sources of knowledge are valued and resourced equally in Indonesia. Many citizen organisations are hesitant to be too closely associated with government. For their part, technocrats, scientists and government decision makers can be reluctant to engage with local knowledge. Consequently, there is mutual distrust that can only be overcome by improved interaction and deepened respect (Guggenheim, 2012; Rakhmani and Siregar, 2016).

This chapter argues that paying attention to local citizen-generated knowledge is crucial for better policy making and democracy by providing context and meaning. A country's knowledge sector can be improved by opening up policy making to citizens and democratising the public sphere. These approaches, as we will see in the empirical chapters, can be more sustainable than top-down development designs of state leaders and experts. This chapter will start with a historical exposé of public decision making and move to how policies are produced. We will then make the case that local knowledge is a prerequisite for democratisation of policy making and the improvement of public policies.

The study of meaning and local knowledge

Definitions of local knowledge are mainly found in anthropological literature. Clifford Geertz (1983) defines local knowledge as knowledge held locally, by local people, a cultural system which becomes common sense for people who share a communal sensibility. The emphasis here is on meaning; the interpretation of culture is 'not an experimental science in search of law but an interpretive one in search of meaning' (Geertz, 1973: 5). Cultural studies of politics and policies argue that beliefs and perceptions are constituent parts of government and policy making. Politics should be viewed not only as competition over scarce resources, but also as representations of historical practices and local knowledge (Cannadine and Price, 1987; Kertzer, 1988; Vincent, 1990; Gledhill, 1994; Schaffer, 1998; Olivier de Sardan, 2005; Bubandt, 2014). Cultural representations are instruments for political discourse. Political symbolism, rituals and normative representation are employed for the legitimate execution of power and domination.

The lack of cultural understanding within a democracy negatively affects its basic meaning: a powerful political imagery of hope and autonomy. To achieve this, 'democracy has to be driven by a "spirit", a secular dream of trust and mutual association by the people and for the people' (Bubandt, 2014: 13). In a study of democracy and violence in Sri Lanka, Jonathan Spencer (2007: 15) notes that something is lost 'if we insist on excluding local meaning from our definition of the political' (see also Schaffer, 1998 for how to understand local forms of democracy in Senegal). In the same vein, the lack of meaning and context negatively affects how policy making is implemented.

While the anthropologist's perspective has provided us with an important understanding of what constitutes local knowledge (the values, beliefs and meanings) and the nature of local knowledge which combines logics of description and logics of prescription (Yanow, 2003), a political-economy analysis of local knowledge requires additional analytical concepts, which help us to analyse and understand whether the production and use of local knowledge are inputs or rather outcomes of the political-economy relations in a society. Distinguishing the political-economy dimensions of local knowledge in its production and use, as well as the relationship between them is important, as contexts vary. Such a perspective addresses:

- What is local?
- Which (local) people are engaged and how?
- Whose definition prevails?
- Who owns what and how do we know they do/do not?
- Who decides local knowledge uptake?
- Who wins, who loses?

On the supply (knowledge production) side, the political-economy dimensions of local knowledge can be analysed from a socio-economic perspective on structure and hierarchies in the community that generates the local knowledge because these are the quintessential manifestations of power that will shape the structure of local knowledge. In this respect, local knowledge is a consequence of power relations in a community; it is produced by and through a given structure and order, and has dominant and subordinate relationships – local knowledge reflects structures of authority and power in a community – the essence of politics. Citizens seldom use local knowledge exclusively; they integrate scientific and professional knowledge from their own lived experience. It is this broader concept of local knowledge that reflects the links between the three types of knowledge, and that plays an important role in the participation of communities in public policy processes.

On the demand (policy making) side, political economy queries are about understanding the incentives or disincentives that favour or hinder the use of local knowledge; this informs what knowledge or intermediary mechanisms are most appropriate for informing and influencing public policy making, as well as why some types of knowledge are more acceptable or suitable than others. Based on case studies from Southeast Asian countries, Pellini et al (2012) present a framework to understand the landscape: technical evidence alone is not effective in influencing the local knowledge-to-policy market. Only an inclusive and inter-disciplinary supply of different types of knowledge by different stakeholders will result in positive outcomes by establishing a more accountable, participatory and transparent local governance environment.

As seen in Figure 1.2, in Chapter One, policy development does not occur in a predictable way. This means that we need to focus on issues of values, context and power, issues that matter to people where they live and work. As we will see in Chapters Four to Six, there are many exciting knowledge initiatives emerging from spontaneous solutions generated by individuals and communities in Indonesia. These can at times be more sustainable than top-down development designs of state leaders and experts. They are based on trial and error, iterations, and adapting to changes in the natural and human-made environment – in short, on local knowledge that emerges from lived experience and practice.

Public decision making, bureaucratic power and local knowledge

Let us now make a quick detour to the historical relationship between public policy and different forms of knowledge, which will allow us to better understand the current importance of local knowledge. The past 50 years have seen the global emergence of three waves of policy making and public management, characterised as, from Rowing to Steering to Serving (Denhardt and Denhardt, 2007).

Both Rowing and Steering gave primacy to the state in public management. In the Rowing phase, following the Second World War, the birth of modern public management was populated by technocrats with thoughts of social engineering. They set the policies and were very much at the top of the pyramid in public management (Weiler, 2009). In the 1980s, 'new public management' emerged to address some of the limitations of the earlier approach (Hood, 1991). It had an emphasis on re-inventing government to adopt a more private sector approach (Osborne and Gaebler, 1993). This Steering phase recognised to some degree that a previous failure had been the lack of a role for the citizen. In the New Public Management, citizens were choosing between public goods, taking a free-market ideology as their basis, although services continued to be designed and delivered by technical specialists in a process that was intended to be mediated by public demand. What this approach failed to realise was that government looks after public as well as private good. This approach could not accommodate public good and therefore largely failed.

These schools of public management failed in part because they did not take local knowledge into account and did not effectively engage the citizenry. Wildavsky and Pressman (1973) make a similar point in their wide-ranging study of policy implementation in the United States. They demonstrate that policy failure at implementation is not only about the complexity of the institutional mechanisms but also that policies designed at the national level in Washington DC do not take into account regional differences, rural–urban differences, and so on. In other words, they do not correspond to the needs of citizens in local communities and are designed without the benefit of citizen input.

Because of what was seen as a failure by new public management to serve the public good, the past two decades have witnessed calls for deepening democracy through a new role for public administrators, transparency of information and social accountability. Sometimes called 'new public service' (Denhardt and Denhardt, 2007) or 'deliberative democracy' (Gastil and Levine, 2005), the focus is on the role of policy making and public management to serve the public, not the other way around. In this deeper engagement of 'co-governance' (Ackerman, 2004), citizens take part in policy making, monitoring and calling service organisations and government to account through a number of mechanisms, for example, ombudsman, mobilisation of the public, mass media or the court system. It moves beyond the 'ritual participation' of the traditional tick-the-box planning process (Cooke and Kothari, 2001; Hickey and Mohan, 2004) and allows for a more constructive role of citizens in monitoring and ensuring that public service standards are reached.

This transition from 'government to governance' has important implications for our discussion of evidence and knowledge. The failures of the old and new public management paradigms are also the failures of the state that focused on limited sources of knowledge. Today, government is no longer the sole holder of knowledge. The question is who owns which knowledge and the issue is the fairness of the contestation of different types of knowledge, both in use for policy as well as in the production of knowledge. Thus, the government's new 'serving' role is, on the one hand, to facilitate and make things happen (being the enabling state, serving the public) and, on the other hand, providing the space for contestation and multiple sources of sets of knowledge. Government officials need to interact with people not as clients or objects but as citizens with rights and holders of valuable local knowledge. The new skills that a government official needs to learn include how to create spaces for citizen involvement in policy decisions and oversight, how to commission (rather than provide) a range of public services, and how to lead negotiations and mobilise consent about desired local policies.

Working politically

Public policy is a political product. To improve the use of local knowledge in public policy making we need to work with local knowledge through its political dimensions. Local knowledge as a shared communal sensibility is a representation of a community's shared concerns or aspirations. From a political perspective, local knowledge is an interest group. Local knowledge falls under one influential definition of interest groups (Martini, 2012: 2): 'any association of individuals or organisations that on the basis of one or more shared concerns, attempts to influence public policy in its favour'. In the context of policy making, we could see local knowledge as a shared political aspiration. In this regard, the domain of contestation is thus not about how to make local knowledge scientific so that it can compete with scientific knowledge in the knowledge hierarchy, but to acknowledge the importance of contestation with other interest groups in influencing policy. Local knowledge producers, as an interest group, may focus on their position as representing public interest and holding local knowledge that will compete with other interests (scientific and professional).

Local knowledge, through a political representation platform, may directly or indirectly influence policy-making processes through intermediary actors (parliament members, civil society actors or even the so-called professional lobbyists) as it seeks to affect legislative action. These attempts to influence policy making may take place through various mechanisms, including direct communication with government officials, participation in public hearings, drafting reports to members of the government on specific policy issues, as well as through social media and setting public discourse in conventional media. In this process, as noted by Bievre (2007), local knowledge should work with different types of knowledge and resources, such as expertise on policy issues, information on the opinions of other policy makers, and community organisers.

Transforming local knowledge into an interest group platform to inform policy is not a corrupt or illegitimate activity.[1] It is about working politically to ensure that the community's shared aspirations are adopted in public policy. Interest group platforms can improve policy making, and they play an important role in holding governments accountable by providing community consent as well pressure in the legislative and regulatory processes. In a decentralised country like Indonesia, interest group influence through lobbying is an alternative instrument of political influence vis-à-vis corruption that is centred around political parties (Keefer, 2002).

It should be noted that the advantages and disadvantages of this platform will depend on how much power such interest groups have,

---

[1] There are debates about the pros and cons of interest groups' influence on policy making (Zinnbauer, 2009; Martini, 2012). Using interest groups to influence the policy process is a key element of the decision-making process. Martini (2012) also describes the advantages and disadvantages of working through interest groups, regarding how much power such interest groups have, and how power is distributed among them.

as well as how power is distributed among them (Martini, 2012). As seen in one case study in this book, disproportionate influence of a dominant clan in a coastal fishery policy in Maluku, for example, could have led to undue influence or elite capture that marginalised other clans; while a male dominated whale hunting industry in Lembata in East Nusa Tenggara may have ignored women's needs or aspirations around participation in whale hunting. The relationship between policy makers and interest groups walks a fine ethical line that separates participatory democracy from undue influence.

The primary focus here is the local knowledge that communities use to influence policy processes. But there are other forms of local knowledge. One of these is religious knowledge, to which we now briefly turn our attention. When we think about processes of using knowledge and evidence, often an underlying assumption is that the types of knowledge that are valid for influencing policy, such as research, data and evidence, are all secular. However, there is also local knowledge that refers to religious scriptures and practices and that can have a positive impact on public policy.

Box 3.1 Religious knowledge as a form of local knowledge[2]

Since the Age of Enlightenment in western thought, the religious has been separated from the secular. The secular has been privileged as the domain of the rational, and the scientific, the modern. The religious is seen as the domain of the mystical, the emotional and the pre-modern. Decades of privileging the secular culminated in the secularisation thesis – that as countries developed, they would secularise. That thesis has now been debunked (Gorski et al, 2012). Empirical evidence shows nation after nation advancing economically and politically, while both public and private attention to religious issues has not diminished at all, but rather increased. Indonesia is a good example of that. Scholars now talk about a 'post-secular world'. A rise of scholarly attention to religion among political scientists and even economists can be noted.

The same phenomenon holds true in the donor world and among those concerned with economic growth and development. In the past this was considered a bastion

[2] Special thanks to Robin Bush for drafting this section of the chapter.

LOCAL KNOWLEDGE IN DEMOCRATIC POLICY MAKING

of secularism, but in the decades of the 2000s, the World Bank, the United Kingdom Department for International Development and other donors have funded research and projects that examined the role of faith and religion in development. This work ranges from instrumental efforts to engage religious communities in development initiatives (something with which Indonesia has a long history), to considerations of how state policies can be influenced by religious communities.

In Asia, political and philosophical thought did not demarcate religion from the secular in the same way that western political thought did, and a much more nuanced and integrated relationship between religion and politics exists. The first principle of the Pancasila, the philosophical foundation of Indonesia, is belief in the One and Only God. In that context, the government of Indonesia recognises six official religions. There is a direct relationship between religion and policy, and, especially, implementation of public services. Indonesian citizens who do not have a KTP (identity card) validating their membership of one of these six religions do not have access to public services, cannot attend public schools, cannot legally marry and cannot register their children's births.[3]

This raises questions about whose religious knowledge matters: who has the authority to determine the borders of those six sanctioned religions? Who is in and who is out? On what religious knowledge is that authority based? These questions are extremely important in determining how public policy is implemented, and they are relevant to the daily lives of citizens depending on those services. Several Indonesian scholars, among them Zainal Abidin Bagir of the University of Gajah Mada, explore the roles of state institutions such as the Ministry of Religious Affairs, quasi state-institutions such as *Majelis Ulama Indonesia* (MUI) or the Indonesian Ulema Council, and non-state organisations such as *Nadlatul Ulama* (NU) and *Muhammadiyah*, in defining religious identity and therefore giving certain citizens access to public services, while excluding others (Bagir, 2014).

In Asia more generally, and in Indonesia in particular, there is a view that as religion permeates daily life at many levels, it should also be considered when developing

[3] The Minister for Home Affairs has publicly declared that citizens do not have to fill in the 'religion' field on their KTP, but this has yet to be formally translated into policy or law, so it is not yet being observed. Furthermore, in November 2017 the Constitutional Court ruled that followers of indigenous faiths do not have to leave the 'religion' field blank on their KTP, in essence constituting recognition by the state of indigenous faiths. Whether this will result in an end to discriminatory policies based on religious affiliation remains to be seen.

and implementing public policy. This level of comfort with a porous relationship between the religious and the political, especially when it comes to policy, allows us to consider religion, and religious knowledge, as one of many factors that we should take into account as we seek to reduce poverty, improve public services, and stimulate economic welfare through public policy. As illustrated in the story of the Muhammadiyah Disaster Management Centre below, Indonesia provides positive examples of how religious knowledge and religious authority can improve access to marginalised communities, enable dissemination of important health and education messages and practices through the vast national networks that religious organisations have, or provide legitimacy to government social policies.

Muhammadiyah Disaster Management Centre

One of the most active and well-known disaster response organisations in Indonesia, the Muhammadiyah Disaster Management Centre (MDMC), is religious-based. After the 2004 Aceh tsunami, Muhammadiyah networks were drawn upon by international and national relief agencies alike, as they were able to move quickly to get in to affected areas. The local communities trusted them more than government, and they could quickly mobilise support, donations and assistance from their massive membership. When this experience was repeated after the 2006 Yogyakarta earthquake, the 2008 Sumatra earthquake and the 2009 Mt Merapi eruption, the Muhammadiyah leadership realised that they could make a unique contribution to disaster response in Indonesia. As a result, they formally established MDMC. MDMC helps to implement Indonesia's disaster response policy, including prevention and mitigation efforts. It provides disaster mitigation training in schools and hospitals all over the country. But how does MDMC use religious knowledge in its work, which is humanitarian response and therefore not religiously based? MDMC has drawn on its religious training to produce several papers such as, 'A theology of disasters', and, 'An ideology of human rights post-disaster'. These papers explore how religious teachings help us understand how to respond in times of disaster, and about people's responsibility to help all humans, regardless of religion. Faith can provide motivation and comfort to people who have lost loved ones or homes in disasters. MDMC uses its unique position as a religious-based disaster-response organisation to bring the two worlds of religious knowledge and disaster policy together in more effective ways.

Local knowledge and participatory development

Citizen participation involves systematic participation in policy formulation and decision making by groups of citizens, linking those who have developed participatory methods for consultation, planning and monitoring to the new governance agenda (Manor, 1998; Blair, 2000; Pimbert, 2001; Fung and Wright, 2003). The goal of citizen engagement is not to ensure that everyone gets what they want all the time, but to change the power relationship to some fairer form of reconciliation of competing claims,[4] and to add more diversity to knowledge claims.

Early participatory development was often measured by popular presence in meetings. A development project would be considered 'participatory' if we could show disaggregated data about the number of community members (by sex, ideally) who attended the project's meetings. This was a very low bar by which to measure participation. The new generation of thinking in participatory development is more on substantial participation and the incorporation of scientific, professional and local knowledge in policy making. In other words, how much is the development process informed by the community's ideas and aspirations: how culturally sensitive, how gender sensitive, how inclusive? Conceptualising the community as the master of the development process, then, is measured more qualitatively in a power-relations framework. Under this new thinking about participatory development, the central factor is not community participation, but democratisation of knowledge: how far local knowledge is appropriated in development decision-making processes. What the people know and have practised over time should be part of the design of policies and projects that seek to empower and develop these people, who are defined as excluded or marginalised.

There is a danger that local knowledge can become elitist when it is used to increase community participation through mobilisation

---

[4] Owen Barder, quoted in http://oxfamblogs.org/fp2p/is-engaging-citizens-a-panacea-a-swindle-or-a-bit-of-both-plus-why-im-excited-about-moocs/.

(Cooke and Kothari, 2001). The institutionalisation of *gampong* in Aceh's administration (see Chapter Four, case study 7) is one such example. Policies, projects and programmes are designed from above. At the local level, local leaders mobilise citizens to participate in the implementation of these programmes just to provide labour or to legitimise operations. Conducive political and ethical conditions for development processes need to be set by:[5]

- seeking the community's consent;
- ensuring community members are adequately informed about the projects under consideration; the information made available is both adequate and relevant, and properly packaged; people are able to make sense of it; and the information can be used as a tool in their decision making;
- challenging peoples' existing representation system so that the project is inclusive;
- ensuring representatives are elected and accountable to the citizens; they represent their community's views and opinions; this political dimension is sometimes neglected in debates on the use of local knowledge in development because local knowledge is perceived as an indigenous mechanism that is not necessarily democratic and inclusive;
- providing a platform for dialogue;
- agreeing on what kind of organisations and communities should have their voices heard; engaging in discussion and decision making that is uninterrupted by a development project's power structure; if the decisions are local-knowledge based, people are not afraid to make whatever proposition they want to make if it is a shared concern in the community.

The other strategic role of local knowledge in democratising the development process is through opening up for inclusive decision

---

[5] Adapted from Laaksonen (2006). Susskind and Cruikshank (2006) present a similar approach in *Breaking Robert's Rules*.

making. Decentralisation is devolution of power. Local knowledge informs the appropriate structure and mechanism for resource management and decision-making processes. The ultimate use of local knowledge in development is empowerment. Here, power is given to the people through using indigenous knowledge and capacities that are available on the ground. These indigenous structures of participation enable people at the community level with the elected representatives to participate in discussions about development problems and their solutions. Local knowledge should be available for different groups of community members so that the local people are able to determine which project they prefer, how resources should be mobilised internally, and what is needed from outside.

Society today is more complex than it was a generation ago. In a lower-middle-income country such as Indonesia, simple development issues have been addressed: building schools and setting a strong education budget, for example. With globalisation and increasing layers of actors in governance, solutions are much more complex: how to get all children through secondary school is not simply a matter of building schools; it requires addressing a multitude of social and economic issues, including ensuring teaching quality, building community priority on education, creating incentives for school attendance, among others. These issues cannot be solved technically (Mangkusubroto et al, 2016). They call for behavioural changes not only in government policies and practices surrounding universal education, but also from parents and teachers. There are multiple layers of governance: Indonesia has recently decentralised decision making to 75,000 villages (Antlov et al, 2016), while at the regional level the country is a member of the ASEAN Free Trade Community and the Trans-Pacific Partnership. Issues such as equitable growth and climate change cannot be addressed by a single line ministry alone. Complexity requires government to change, using multiple sources of knowledge and data to find proper solutions.

New governance structures and citizen demands can compel government agencies to expand public consultations, implement participatory governance practices at the local level, encourage popular participation, and develop new partnerships with civil society organisations – the New Public Service. Governance, policy and politics are no longer only for specialised experts, politicians and government officials. This requires a 'de-professionalisation' of politics and public administration (Fischer, 2009), or in the words of Harry Boyte (2004: xi), 'breaking the tyranny of technique'. In a more positive light, it is the democratisation of public policy, involving citizens in public policies, decision making and the knowledge-to-policy process.

We thus need to broaden the role of citizens and local knowledge beyond that of being objects of state policy, passive recipients of government funding or quaint producers of local wisdom. The disillusion with mainstream politics is something we have seen in Europe and the United States over the past decades. As mentioned, this has given birth to new forms of populism, citizen politics, deliberative democracy and everyday governance experiments. Interestingly, just as in Indonesia, it seems that the most exciting developments are happening at the local level, because that is where the density of social forces is to be found and where political recruitment and the building of constituencies takes place. It is also where people can translate national policies into local programmes and where local issues relate to national ideology.

Scientific knowledge can only add value if the experts producing it understand the meaning and the local context. If 'what matters is what works' (Tony Blair, quoted in Banks, 2009: 1), we need local knowledge to show what works under what conditions and for whom. It is not the policy solution that is the end; it is actually making policies work – and this is where the donor community has often failed in promoting locally sensitive solutions. This is all the more true if we are looking at policy ideas that inherently are about political choices and preferences. Policy without local knowledge will be ill targeted and random, and impact may be positive, neutral or negative. Enriching policies by incorporating local knowledge contributes to the testing and factual observation that is at the core of knowledge generation for national development.

Conclusion

The new governance paradigm introduced in this chapter is about process, politics and context. Through participation of citizens and the integration of local knowledge in policy making, a connection between the community and public good is made. It allows citizens as users to have a more direct, informed and creative say in rewriting the policies by which public services are designed and delivered. That requires a democratisation of the public policy-making process, in which citizens participate not only during elections but also on everyday issues. Power is generated by citizen action. Sustainable political action begins with 'a thousand tiny empowerments', not grand designs (Sandercock, 1998).

Policy making is inherently political: 'Values, interests, personalities, timing, circumstance and happenstance – in short, democracy – determine what actually happens' (Banks, 2009: 4). We must investigate issues that matter in the locality in which we live (Flyvbjerg, 2001: 166). If it is true that as Peter Drucker famously said, 'culture eats strategy for breakfast, lunch and dinner', it behoves us to give closer consideration to the social meanings and context that make up context and culture – otherwise we will end up with picture-perfect policies that might fail in implementation. When research influences policy, as noted by Carden (2009: 50), 'it is always in the turbulent confluence of factors that shape policy decisions and policy outcomes'. And in this turbulence, we need to be guided by the knowledge and context created by local communities and citizens.

FOUR

Stories of local knowledge

In 2014, KSI awarded ten grants to Indonesian research institutions to write up their stories on local knowledge, specifically on how local knowledge is generated, managed and used for influencing policy and community practice.[1] In April 2016, a conference was organised, ahead of which KSI asked the ten organisations to write a short story about their experiences.[2] Before we move into more detail about how local knowledge is generated and used, this chapter will give a brief overview of these cases to provide a bit of context and flavour to the more analytical chapters to follow. We base these stories on the summary reports of the organisations prepared ahead of the conference.

---

[1] Of the more than 500 proposals received, 74 per cent came from NGOs and 21 per cent from universities (the remaining were individuals and government agencies). There were 31% per cent based in Java and 7 per cent were from Maluku and Papua. The remaining proposals were divided evenly between Sumatra, Kalimantan, Sulawesi and West and East Nusa Tenggara.

[2] See www.ksi-indonesia.org/en/news/detail/knowledge-sector-initiative-ksi-supports-local-knowledge-in-policy-making

Case study 1: Water for all – *Perkumpulan Pikul* (Pikul Association)

In 2010, the villagers of Baumata Timur village in East Nusa Tenggara received great news. The government's Community-based Drinking Water and Sanitation Provision Programme, or *Penyediaan Air Minum dan Sanitasi Berbasis Masyarakat* (*PAMSIMAS*) was coming to their village. Goodbye water crisis! This project successfully built four new water reservoirs, including a reservoir from the local Baumata water source; it rehabilitated four reservoirs that were inherited and abandoned by another project in 2006; and it expanded the piping network by around 500 metres. To distribute water, an electrical pump with a capacity of 13,000 Kwh was installed. The total cost of this project amounted to Rp 275 million (US$20,600), with funding from the national budget (APBN), local budget (APBD) and the community itself. However, since the completion of this project in December 2010, the long-awaited water never came. The electrical metre on the pump has already been removed by the electric company.

Many locations in the province of East Nusa Tenggara share similar stories.[3] Government projects to provide clean water or irrigation systems often end badly. Currently, East Nusa Tenggara experiences a water deficit of around 1.5 billion cubic metres per year. The water needs of only 36 per cent of the population have been met. The provincial government has set a target that by 2019, the water needs of everyone will be fulfilled. Technically and hydrologically, it is feasible to meet the water needs of the people with the water resources in the province. But why are so many water provision projects not sustainable? What is wrong? And what is the solution? The Kupang-based NGO Pikul believes one of the reasons is that very little is known about the

---

[3] Despite a series of infrastructure projects in this province, one of Indonesia's poorest, low rainfall and poor infrastructure cause water crises every year in the dry season. This forces local communities to consume unhygienic water, as residents cannot afford local tap water at exorbitant prices. Further, water shortages in the province can take a heavy toll on rice cultivation and irrigation, leading to harvest failures (Asian Development Bank, 2012).

local socio-political factors that may be constraining the sustainability of water management initiatives in East Nusa Tenggara.

According to the province's 2014–2019 development plan, at least ten dams/aqueducts, 200 irrigations dams and 4,000 small dams will be constructed by the government. Looking at the case of the Kolhua Dam, in the city of Kupang, the development plan may not be easy to realise. Kolhua Dam, which cost Rp 480 billion (US$36 million), incited protests and conflicts due to land acquisition issues. This is only one dam which required just 81 hectares of land. The land needed to build ten dams is in the order of 15,490 hectares. It is hard to imagine that this will be feasible in the near future.

To explore this challenge, Pikul conducted research in a number of locations in East Nusa Tenggara where communities have successfully managed water resources for their own needs using local knowledge and wisdom-based approaches. The research was carried out in several communities and a variety of approaches were identified. In Naip village, for example, communities successfully engaged in clan-based water management; in Apui, the community approach to managing water was church-based; in Noelbaki, the community used interest group-based water management; in Uiasa, a village-based water management approach was used; and in Wehali, indigenous community-based water management was practised.

Pikul found that there were ten principles of using local knowledge needed so that the supply of water would flow to all parts of the community. The most important of these were:[4]

---

[4] The other six principles are: 1) staged sanction policy (sanction for the violators will be given in stages), 2) affordable conflict resolution mechanism, 3) recognition of rights to organise, 4) community-based hierarchical management, 5) community engagement, and 6) water governance reflects the socio-cultural structure.

1. The community agrees that even though the water is underneath the land or an area belonging to a certain clan, it will still be collectively used and managed. The ownership of water resources is not based on personal claim but will always be under the control of clans.
2. As a source of life and myths, water resources are closely linked to the indigenous structure of the local community. The relationship between water and people lies within a local system/institution. For example, water in the context of the Wehali group is related to a supernatural force, *Wematan Maromak*, which is the origin of the local people. Indigenous relationships or structures in connection with water sub-systems are symbolised by indigenous houses. These act as a collective reminder of the structure and process of water management according to the beliefs of the local people.
3. As an identity within which rests the knowledge and various local wisdom values, water resources are physically managed in accordance with local beliefs. In Naip and Wehali, water owners or controllers do not wish to physically change to a more modern system, such as creating reservoirs. However, in Noelbaki, Uiasa and Apui, there have been efforts to create physical change by building reservoirs and using other forms of water capture. Despite differences in the capture systems, one thing remains the same: the management structure remains in the hands of the clan who discovered the water.
4. Water resource management revolves around specific boundaries in terms of owner clans, myths, epics and the stories behind the water source. Also, there are clear rituals and regulations related to its management and use, identification of beneficiaries, and the physical boundaries of the water supply. The procedures and structures of water management become a collective memory for the local people, a form of acknowledgement and responsibility over existing resources.

Pikul made local wisdom a reference for its recommendation to the local government's obligation to meet the people's rights to water.

It successfully inserted the idea of local knowledge in the debate on water management. Six policy briefs were developed and disseminated to trigger local discourse and policy dialogue.[5] The Drinking Water and Environmental Health Working Group (*Pokja AMPL*) of the public works office, which is a multi-party working group managing drinking water and environmental health affairs, has shown an interest in disseminating Pikul's findings.

Case study 2: 'Baleo! Baleo! Baleo!' – Poros Photo

The 'Baleo! Baleo! Baleo!' call marks the beginning of whale fishing parties in Lamalera, a small village on the island of Lembata, East Nusa Tenggara.[6] The people of Lamalera move swiftly to the beach facing the Sawu Sea. They know that the 'godsend gift' has arrived in the sea: whales.

When the whales arrive, the *peledangs*, the traditional Lamalera fishing boat that can accommodate 16 men, are prepared. The *matros* or ship crews stand by in position. The fishers, along with their spears, known as *lefa alap,* enter the *peledang. Leo*, or ropes, kept in their traditional houses are carried on their shoulders – this is the origin of the term '*baleo*'. *Lamafa,* the spearmen carrying the *leo* are prepared to command the ships.

Prayers are offered, then the *peledang* are pushed into the ocean. Traditional songs are sung to lift the spirits of brave men sailing the sea. And so the hunt begins. Good cooperation and a clear division of roles between *peledang* crews and between *peledangs* contribute to a high success rate in whale spearing. In addition, there is a belief that peace on the land makes for good hunting from the sea. If a *matros*

---

[5] These six policy briefs (in Indonesian language) are available at www.perkumpulanpikul.org/2016/02/ diseminasi-riset-air/

[6] Lamalera is a village of around 2,000 people. It is located on the stony island of Lembata and has very little agriculture. The population depends on resources from the sea and many communities on Lembata hunt whales for subsistence living (Barnes, 1984; Fortier, 2014).

sails without making peace with his family or enemy, his boat will face problems during the hunt.

There are tensions, however, involved in whaling and commercial tourism. To support the local whaling communities, Poros Photo decided to communicate the message that this tradition was integral to the community's way of life and indeed its world view; abolishing it would end not only their livelihood, but the very thing upon which their sense of community and identity is built. A photo and film exhibition was organised and a photo essay book was published to communicate the message that the indigenous practice of community whaling is different from commercial whaling.

Community-based whaling is a centuries-old tradition which is still practised in Lamalera today.[7] Usually, whales 'anchor' here from April to November on their migration between the Indian and Pacific Oceans. When these giant sea creatures pass Sawu Sea, right in front of the entrance to Lembata island, the hunt for whales begins. Only sperm whales (*Physeter macrocphalus*) are hunted. Seguni whales are not hunted because they are too fierce, while blue whales are believed to be the guardians of Lamalera. 'We do not hunt blue whales because it is forbidden by our ancestors', the fishers said.

The distribution of the hunting yield is a tradition passed down from generation to generation, based on local wisdom. All the Lamalera people obey this distribution system, ensuring that there is no argument over the bounty from the hunt. The distribution follows the social structure of the community. It begins with landlords, the owners of houses located where the ships first catch fish, then the ship owners, followed by spearmen, and then the rest of the people. 'Everybody gets their share', said Bona Bedding, a local fisher and community organiser. Ship owners still remember the kindness of people who gave them wood to make *peledang*. Bona remembered being told by his father to give meat to someone whose trees are cut to make ships.

---

[7] According to Barnes (1984), an anonymous Portuguese document of 1624 describes the islanders as hunting whales with harpoons for their oil, and implies that they collected and sold ambergris.

Everyone has the opportunity to obtain a share of each captured whale. Not only men who joined the expedition, but also widows, unmarried women, and wives whose husbands can no longer sail or do not have the opportunity to spear, receive a share. In order to receive a blessing from the sea, the community exchanges goods. Therefore, it is not surprising that when the whale is cut (when the community sharing mechanism is completed), there are women sitting next to it with containers filled with goods that can be exchanged for whale meat.

This process illustrates that the hunting yield distribution system is based on communal cultural values as opposed to accumulated economic values. As part of a larger economic system, whale meat is also kept as 'savings' for major events, such as marriages or deaths. What is more important is that whale jerky becomes an exchange coin in Lamalera, sometimes serving as the main barter tool. Merchants in market places tend to prioritise bartering over 'the power of cash' or selling and purchasing for people coming to the market.

Poros Photo went beyond the simple documentation of local observations and knowledge by using interactive exhibitions and multimedia. This presented new possibilities for recording and sharing local observations and knowledge. The audio and video recordings documented observations, knowledge and narratives as told by knowledge holders and communities in the language of the local community and was able to highlight the importance of respecting community-based whaling.

Case study 3: *Pranata Mangsa*: When traditional knowledge meets science – Centre for Anthropological Studies, University of Indonesia (PUSKA UI)

Climate change can trigger a domino effect in the world's atmosphere. El Niño, which hit Africa in February 2015, has left a drought in its wake. However, the devastation of El Niño did not stop there. The dry season in several tropical regions, such as Indonesia, is getting increasingly worse. FAO stated that in 2015 and 2016, El Niño brought the worst drought in 35 years.

Farmers are one group directly affected by climate change. A long dry season, an erratic rainfall rate and hot temperatures result in confusion in the planting pattern which they have used for so long. 'We can feel the climate change. The heat is unbearable now', said Yusup, a rice farmer in Indramayu on the north coast of West Java, in early April 2016. Although Indramayu is a primary national source of rice production, it remains one of the poorest areas in Java where the majority of the farmers are landless and get little benefit from rice production. People's livelihoods have gradually changed to non-agricultural, with a very high migration rate, both through urbanisation and for cheap migrant labour in East Asia and the Middle East.

The sub-district of Balongan in Indramayu experienced harvest failure at the end of 2015 due to the lack of rain and the absence of other water sources. According to Yusup, climate change has decreased the rainfall rate in Indramayu. The rainy period has also shifted. 'Rain usually starts to fall in October, but this year (2015), the rainy season only began at the end of November', Yusup said. The Meteorology, Climatology and Geophysics Agency later issued a statement that the planting season for 2015 was delayed due to the shift in the rainy season.

Most farmers rely on traditional calculations to determine the planting season. Farmers in Indramayu are familiar with the farming calendar known as *pranata mangsa*.[8] Farmers in East Lombok call it the *warige*, a farming guideline which uses the lunar calendar, according to Hijriyah month. The type of rain that will fall is decided by looking at on which day the Muslim day one of Muharram falls. This system

---

[8] *Pranata Mangsa* originates from two words, *pranata*, which means regulation, and *mangsa*, which means season or time. So, *pranata mangsa* is a regulation used by farmers to decide on or carry out their work. This was initiated by King Pakubuwono VII and began to be used on 22 June 1856. This system is used, for example, to conduct agricultural-related business such as farming, or for fishing, travelling outside of the home region, and going to war. *Pranata mangsa* is a seasonal time regulation based on the solar calendar.

is handed down from generation to generation and uses natural signs like the position of stellar constellations and animal behaviour to determine the planting season.

The problem is, climate change has rendered traditional systems like *pranata mangsa* and *warige* inapplicable. Yusup said that the calculation of the planting season in *pranata mangsa* could be far different from the actual conditions. 'When the planting season should have begun, there is still long drought', said Yusup. 'Farmers need to learn to adapt.' In principle, farmers are true learners. From year to year, season to season and day to day, they learn from their planting processes, from successes and from failures. They also learn from elders and wise people sharing their experiences. They share knowledge and learn from each other. Some farmers realise the situation has changed. 'I am 50 years old, and this is the first year I have experienced no rain during *Bau Nyale*', said a farmer in East Lombok. *Bau Nyale* is a folk festival that celebrates the annual appearance of the *nyale* sea worms. Hordes of people flock to the sea to catch these rare creatures. 'Usually, people would get soaked when they want to take *nyale*', the farmer continued.[9] Meanwhile, farmers who usually plant their crop based on a planting calendar can no longer use one, as the estimations of the planting season are incorrect.

Official farmer schools, *Penyuluh Pertanian Lapangan* (PPL), have existed for some time through government-led outreach programmes. However, the approach was a top-down model which lasted for only one planting season and only covered certain areas of land during training. Siregar and Crane (2011) reported that locally specific conditions, such as social and technical conditions of agricultural production, influence farmers' ability and willingness to apply seasonal climate forecasts provided through PPL schools. Field schools

---

[9] The indigenous Sasak population in East Lombok believe that *Bau Nyale* is a sign that the rainy season is about to begin. But in 2015, this ritual was not followed by rain, and there were no worms. Thousands of people gathered waiting for worms to rise to the sea surface, but only a few of them went home with *nyale*.

have blossomed since the Green Revolution was initiated in 1970s. Unfortunately, this revolution also caused farmers to rely more on commercial agricultural packages (seeds, fertilisers and pesticides). The top-down model does not work well for local farmers. They want sustainable, participatory field schools and have therefore developed Farmers Clubs and Rainfall Observation Clubs. They will not believe something until they have seen the proof. Participatory experiments between scientists and farmers, as well as among farmers, are needed to find planting methods that are adaptive to climate change.

Since 2009, the Indramayu Farmers' Club, facilitated by PUSKA UI, has learned about agro-meteorology at science field shops (*Warung Ilmiah Lapangan*). Several farmer groups, local NGOs and agro-meteorology experts from Indonesia, the Netherlands and Africa have also collaborated through this programme. In early 2015, a similar programme was introduced to farmers in East Lombok, also a very poor district with similar migration issues.

Learning to monitor and calculate rainfall helps farmers respond to climate change. Working with PUSKA UI, a number of communities have combined scientific methods with monitoring rice field conditions, animal behaviour, pests and plant diseases that they routinely record. 'This monitoring results in planting period estimations', said Yusup, a member of the Indramayu Rainfall Observation Club. Farmers are developing new behaviour: they have become researchers. Farmers who previously carried hoes now also carry pens and books. Measuring rainfall and observing rice field ecosystems can help farmers determine the timing of the planting season. This method is practised every day by farmers in Indramayu and Lombok Timur. 'This is an adaptation strategy to deal with climate change', said Yusup.

'We measure rainfall.' This is how the farmers identify themselves as members of the Indramayu Rainfall Observation Club, an association, network and organisation where farmers throughout sub-districts in Indramayu come to learn agro-meteorology. In the seven years since they were first introduced in Indramayu district, West Java province, science field shops have been established as social institutions for learning agro-meteorology. Science field shops are a new approach to education, an arena where farmers, scientists and educators engage in a knowledge exchange dialogue. Through this exchange, knowledge is transferred from scientists to famers to be used operationally by farmers as active observers and learners. Farmers observe rainfall and agro-ecosystem conditions every day, measure rainfall, document the results, and analyse, discuss and evaluate them together.

In Lombok, farmers call the place where people gather socially *berugaq*. People meet at least once per month to discuss rainfall measurement results, agro-system observations and seasonal scenarios. Scientists or guides provide services that enable new agro-meteorological knowledge to be implemented by farmers. These knowledge transfer and communication technologies include rainfall measurement, comparison of harvest yield and distribution efforts. Scientists learn ways to better operationalise science and combine traditional or local knowledge with scientific knowledge.

This science field shops approach is very different from the government outreach programme, which has a top-down approach. Science field shops provide an interactive learning arena between farmers and facilitators, discussing traditional knowledge, empirical knowledge and scientific knowledge. It is not oriented towards 'aid' or 'a project', but instead focuses on 'farmer empowerment' based on actual conditions and farmers' needs, and is thus much more effective. Local governments in Indramayu and East Lombok have been talking about institutionalising the field shops, something that PUSKA UI is excited about.

Case study 4: Fish sovereignty in *sasi lompa*, Haruku – Centre for Regional Studies and Information (PATTIRO), Jakarta

The marine resources in eastern Indonesia are very rich but are under severe pressure, particularly from destructive fishing techniques that have been used since the 1980s. Economic pressure and market demand provide a strong incentive for further expansion of fisheries. Traditional fisher-farmers with low-technology boats and fishing gear and limited formal education have to compete with commercial vessels carrying younger and stronger fishers. At the same time, enforcement of national fisheries regulations is lax. As well, there are serious deficiencies in government management agencies in terms of motivation, coordination, knowledge, infrastructure and funding. Local village institutions, while generally well respected, have less credence with the younger, commercially oriented fishers (Novaczek et al, 2001: 5). A collapsing economy among local fisher-farmers and competition among community groups have created a situation where conflict within communities[10] and with commercial sectors is inevitable if management and conflict resolution arrangements are not put in place.

To manage these challenges, in the district of Central Maluku, communities are relying on *sasi*, a series of regulations and sanctions governing natural resources and life in the region. In various community groups in Central Maluku, *sasi* has even become a part of religion in their lives. *Sasi* is divided into four types: sea *sasi*, domestic *sasi*, river *sasi* and forest *sasi*. Each *sasi* contains different regulations and sanctions. The sanction is established by *Saniri*, or the Indigenous Council, whose membership consists of representatives from five *soa* (tribes). The enforcement is upheld by *Kewang*, the traditional institution in charge of supervising the implementation of *sasi* rules. 'The King has established *sasi* since the old times', said Vecky Saijka, an inhabitant of the island of Haruku.

To highlight this important local practice, PATTIRO documented the ritual and process of *sasi*, and did an analysis of the key actors involved in the events and their specific roles. They facilitated a number of meetings that agreed on recommendations from the study, to be converted into an academic paper to gain a comprehensive and deep understanding of the concept, objective and goals.

---

[10] With a history of communal religious-associated conflict in Maluku, increasing numbers of Muslim fishers in Christian-dominated areas on the island of Haruku may trigger other communal conflicts. For short but substantive overviews of the origin of sectarian conflict in Maluku in 1999, see van Klinken (2000) and Goss (2000).

Haruku island is one of the sub-districts in Central Maluku that upholds *sasi*. Statistics in 2012 recorded the population of Haruku at just over 30,000 people. There, the most popular *sasi* is *sasi lompa*, namely *sasi* that governs the people who cultivate and harvest *lompa* fish (*Trisina baelama*) living in the Learisa Kayeli river and Maluku sea. '*Sasi lompa* was made to keep people from being hungry', said Soleman Latuharhary, 'but also to protect the sea from being depleted.' *Sasi lompa* is a combination of sea *sasi* and river *sasi* to regulate the aquaculture of *lompa* fish. In the daytime (from 4:30 am to 6:30 pm), the *lompa* and *make* fish are in the Learisa river, 1,500 metres from the estuary. Overnight, the *lompa* and *make* fish swim down the estuary to the sea to find more plankton.

That is why there are two *sasi* in *sasi lompa*. If the fish are at sea, the community uses sea *sasi*. This *sasi* restricts people from capturing *lompa* in the inner sea. Fish can only be captured from the coast in water as deep as the waist. This *sasi* also forbids people from damaging reefs where *lompa* fish live. In some areas, damage is caused by using dynamite to catch *lompa*.

When the fish are in the river, the community implements river *sasi*, which restricts the capture of *lompa* using nets or bore (fish poison). This *sasi* also regulates river traffic. The people are forbidden from using motorised boats in the river, as the oil spill and waste will kill juvenile fish and plankton. People are restricted from capturing another fish if there is a *lompa* fish nearby.

Lompa fish can be harvested or collected at least three times a year. The ceremony is called 'closing the *sasi*', which is symbolised by closing the estuary to fishing, and 'opening the *sasi*', which means people can harvest as much *lompa* fish as they want. This ceremony involves people from all tribes. 'Closing the *sasi*' is usually held in April or May, when the fish can be seen in abundance, gathering around the shore. When this happens, people are restricted from taking a large number of fish, both from the river and from the sea.

After 'closing the *sasi*', the event continues with '*hot sasi*'. This is an event to call fish to go into the river. It starts at 2 am with prayers led by the head of the *Kewang* who is also responsible for punishing or disciplining citizens violating these rules. Afterwards, the head of the *Kewang*, followed by others, burns coconut leaves to attract fish and walks towards the Kewang Rocks at the river, accompanied by music from a drum. When the drum stops, they then shout out, '*Sirewei!*' which means a promise and vow. Then the head of the *Kewang* conveys his speech to the community and pays respect to the ancestors, other living creatures and the spirits. During this time, 'closing the *sasi*' is officially implemented.

Over the next five to seven months, 'opening the *sasi*' is held, usually every Friday. Specific to 'opening the *sasi*', the traditional Haruku King holds the veto right to decide on the time to harvest fish. Other indigenous officials only manage the event. 'The king decides after consulting with government officials, not the *Kewang*', said Vecky Saijka. The time and the amount of fish are two things considered by the king when determining the right time to 'open the *sasi*'.

For years, the *sasi lompa* has been obeyed. As a result, during the opening and closing events people can harvest many tons of fish. The revenue from harvesting fish strengthened the economy of the people on Haruku. With the appropriate harvesting pattern governed by *sasi*, they have maintained supply, while neighbouring islands are becoming over-fished.

The community, however, sometimes disobeys *sasi lompa*, especially youths or outsiders. The people often see motorised boats crossing the river and disturbing fish. Youths sometimes violate *sasi* and keep taking fish even during the 'closing the *sasi*' period. The reported violations mainly result in first and second warnings. However, if violations occur for a third time, the *Saniri*, the indigenous people's council, will call the offender to account. 'We will summon the reporting party to give testimony, so we don't decide the verdict right away. We give opportunity because offenders have the right to defend themselves. It is up to them whether their defence makes sense or not. The witnesses will also be asked for their testimony', said Eliza Kissya, an indigenous *Kewang* leader.

Case study 5: The river that brings life to the city – Institute for Islamic and Society Studies (LK3), Banjarmasin, South Kalimantan

'The Martapura River is calm.
Ships are going back and forth on the stream.'

This is the first line of the traditional *Banjar* folk song, *Sungai Martapura*. From Riam Kanam dam in the district of Banjar (South Kalimantan), the Martapura river flows 17 kilometres, dividing the city of Banjarmasin before merging with the much larger Barito river. 'A place of daily livelihood before returning home', continues the song. This is the closing song in a documentary film, 'Our River, Our Life' made by the Institute for Islamic and Society Studies or *Lembaga Kajian Keislaman dan Kemasyarakatan* (LK3).

The Martapura river is one of the main priorities of the LK3 team, because the course of this river is central to the life of both the city of Banjarmasin and the surrounding district. The Banjar is an ethnic group of around 3.5 million people in southern Kalimantan, including in Banjarmasin, the capital of South Kalimantan. Portions of Banjarmasin are below sea level, so the city rises and falls with the tide. *Lanting* (houses on stilts) line the multiple waterways, which crisscross the city. Taking a small *klotok* (motorised boat) around the rivers and canals reveals a wide variety of activity: people bathing, washing laundry, gossiping, and buying fruit, vegetables and fish from female vendors in small canoes (Sjamsuddin, 2016).

The Martapura delta is considered the centre of the city and is the source of livelihood for the people. Society depends on the Martapura river as it serves as a means of transportation and interaction, irrigation, drainage, ecological and water resources for settlements. The main problem is that the river is heavily polluted due to deforestation and poor sanitation, causing economic and ecological losses.

The deterioration of rivers in Banjarmasin is exacerbated by local governments who ignore local wisdom. The objective of LK3's documentary film of Martapura and its people was to highlight to all parties, be they community or local government, the importance of rivers in the lives of Banjar people and the importance of local wisdom in their management.

The history of the Banjar people is the history of the river. Before the establishment of the Banjar Sultanate at the estuary of the Barito river in the 16th century, each villager named his or her river care community group based on the direction of the river flow. *Sei* – water or river in Banjar language – became the 'spirit' of their life. Unfortunately, this centre of people's lives is increasingly ignored and shrinking, and some of the rivers are experiencing sedimentation. This clearly affects the lives of people who use the river as their means of livelihood.

In addition to being a river community, Banjar people have a very strong religious culture and background. Therefore, a theological approach is very important to encourage participation in activities to save the river environment. By collaborating with religious and indigenous figures, LK3 strives, on one hand, to bring back awareness of local wisdom in Banjarmasin, and on the other hand, to make theology more than a normative issue.

First are the myths of ghosts living in the river, such as a fat creature (*tambun*) living in the whirlpool, a yellow alligator, and a water ghost (*hantu banyu*). According to most people, these myths are passed on from generation to generation, from parents to children. The people realise that the myths, which travel by word of mouth, protect the river, especially by preventing people from throwing garbage into it.

The second aspect of local wisdom is traditional songs and poems that show the bond between the people and the river. These are sung and read during fishing trips or to praise the river. An example is the *Sungai Martapura* song at the beginning of this story. In addition to being a place which supports livelihood, this song gives the Martapura river pride of place for Banjar people, a beautiful site during the night, with abundant local fish: *jelawat*, *puyau* and *sanggiringan*. Unfortunately, the importance of this song fades as the fish decrease and the river is damaged.

The third aspect of local wisdom is the presence of *lanting* houses – floating houses with bamboo flooring. During the golden era of the Banjar Sultanate, these houses served as resting places for merchants.

They also became places for merchants to interact and conduct transactions. Today, their function has even expanded to be a place for fishers to live. *Lanting* houses represent the identity of the Banjar people and are an important medium to unite them. Thus, they should be preserved as part of Banjar people's culture. However, the Banjarmasin city government views *lanting* houses as clutter, and feels that they should be torn down. The people argue that *lanting* houses should be viewed not only on the physical level, but also in terms of the social and cultural values attached to the community.

LK3 held hearings at the Banjarmasin House of Representatives (DPRD) and cooperated with several local government agencies in public discussions, seminars and television talk shows to raise awareness of the importance of river revitalisation and its contribution to local wisdom. The networking and advocacy prowess of LK3 led to an opportunity for community groups to criticise and provide inputs to the government in relation to river revitalisation in Banjarmasin. As a result, the government has established a community-based river care committee.

Interestingly, the effort to learn about these songs and poems has raised people's awareness of the importance of revitalising the river and becoming culturally, religiously and environmentally friendly. Together, people cleaned the river of any waste that polluted it or caused sedimentation. They did this with the intention of obtaining clean water and abundant fish, as in the past. This initiative continued for some weeks, as people realised that cleaning the river could not be done just once, but must be done continuously in order to restore its function.

Case study 6: Wisdom fends off disaster in Pakis village – Bandung Institute for Governance Studies (BIGS)

> 'This is our village.
> Our village, located on the slope of the mountain.
> There are fields, hills, but the forest is bare.'

This narration opens an animated movie by BIGS, 'Preserve Our Forest' (https://youtu.be/RBVuii4REkQ). This eight-minute video is about disasters that occur due to the barren forest, from landslides to floods. The image switches from showing an area affected by disaster to a different community. In this village, there are rice fields and hills. It is also located on the slope of a steep mountain. The difference is that the forest is still intact. Even though the images are animated, the village truly exists. This is the village of Pakis in the district of Kendal, Central Java. It is here that BIGS went to investigate how local knowledge supported the preservation of the Merangan forest around the village.

Merangan is classified as a community forest or *hutan rakyat*, owned by private smallholder farmers. This type of forest is mainly located on Java. Its ecological and sociological landscape is totally different from forest plantations, which are mainly located outside of Java. In densely populated areas such as the districts of Kendal and other forested areas on Java, community forests are located in hilly areas surrounded by state forests, managed by the state forest company, *Perhutani* (Bratamihardja et al, 2005). The daily livelihoods of villagers depend on a combination of agriculture and forestry, but as the forests are controlled by *Perhutani*, farmers are often unsure of their income.

Besides conducting research and systematising local knowledge among the people of Pakis village, BIGS disseminated the findings to villagers in surrounding areas and to policy makers, by exploring and exposing the local wisdom of Pakis. This was not only useful for the people around Pakis and Kendal, but for people in many forests in other locations, especially in densely populated areas like Java. They were able to learn from the experiences of Pakis in managing its forest.

BIGS found there were patterns of behaviour among the people of Pakis when supporting forest conservation, using both traditional and contemporary local knowledge. There were different ways in which local knowledge contributed to preserving the Merangan forest.

Local knowledge has been passed down across generations through stories of heroism by village ancestors when trying to manage the water flow. These heroic stories are closely related to restrictions upheld by the villagers. Restrictions include a ban on cutting trees in the forest and encouragement to harvest forest products only as needed. There is also a restriction prohibiting villagers from entering the forest on certain days.

A second way local knowledge contributes to sustaining the forest is the harmonious behaviour of the people, who are closely connected to nature. A third way is an agreement between farmers and *Perhutani* not to damage the forest. This agreement is enforced using the traditional *rikuh* (shame) culture. As a result, although the Forest Community Organisation is inactive and the forest ranger is not always available to supervise, villagers do not damage the forest because they do not want to be shamed.

BIGS brought these findings to the animated film, 'Preserve Our Forest' to be used as a basis for dissemination and advocacy to other villages around Pakis in Kendal and Semarang. Based on the film, BIGS conducted external validation of the research done in Pakis and collected responses to the film from villagers who attended the screening. BIGS asked villagers how the film was linked to forest conservation in their regions.

After these activities there was a grand event in mid-February 2016 to pay respect to the water springs, and to serve as a reminder of the important role the forest plays in preserving these springs. The ceremony, *Susuk Wangan*, was very festive, with villagers participating from all around Pakis and officials from villages, sub-districts and local government agencies in the province of Central Java and the districts of Semarang and Kendal. Through this ceremony, villagers were reminded of the importance of forest preservation, and especially the importance of local knowledge in this preservation effort.

BIGS identified the inaugural ceremony as a symbolic change in behaviour from the old traditions and habits (local knowledge) related to natural and environmental preservation. Previously, only a handful of villagers would get involved in environmental events (water springs and forests) as they did not feel that they were relevant to their lives, and because some believed the tradition violated religious (Islamic) norms (*bid'ah*).

The presence of officials from outside the programme area at the *Susuk Wangan* ceremony showed that forest conservation in Pakis is not limited along administrative lines. The attendance of government officials and figures indicated that the local government understands the importance of local knowledge, existing traditions and practices within the community. The positive support and response of the local government to this traditional event will continue, with the adoption of principles of local knowledge in local policy-making processes regarding forest conservation. This would be a significant change.

Case study 7: Revitalising *Keujruen Blang* – Centre for Education and Community Studies (PKPM), Aceh

Pangulee hareuket meugoe
'The most important work is farming'

This proverb describes the importance of rice fields for the Acehnese. While praying (*shalat*) is the main worship activity, working in a rice field is the main means of livelihood. Like many other ethnic groups in Indonesia, the Acehnese has its own special indigenous organisation to manage rice fields, called *Keujruen Blang*.

Keujruen Blang comes from the words *keurajeun* or kingdom, meaning territorial power, and *blang,* which means rice field. *Keujruen Blang* can be interpreted as power in the rice field. This also suggests that *Keujruen Blang* has existed since imperial times in Aceh. 'Their duty was to regulate water all the way to giving the order on when to start the planting season', said Syamsulrizal, the Vice District Head of Aceh Besar.

In the local government structure, *Keujruen Blang* is an indigenous institution tasked with assisting *keuchik*,[11] the head of *gampong* (village),

---

[11] The leader of a *gampong adat* community who administers a legal community below the level of sub-district (called *gampong* or equivalent to village) preserves customary *adat* law, social peace, order, accord, amity and welfare. The *keuchik* are directly responsible to the head of the sub-district government (*camat*).

and *Imuem mukim,* the leader of *mukim* (a community unit between sub-district and village level) in agriculture. As an indigenous institution, the management of *Keujruen Blang* is not appointed by the head of the village (*keuchik*) but elected by farmers through discussion.

The structure of *Keujruen Blang* is tiered. At the *mukim* level (an administrative area consisting of several *gampong* and under a sub-district) it is called *Keujruen Cheik*. At the *gampong* or village level, it is called *Keujruen Muda*. If the rice field in the *gampong* is large, there is also *Peutua Blang*, which acts as the 'assistant' for *Keujruen Muda.*

Not all areas in Aceh practice these traditions, not even in Aceh Besar. To most, *Keujruen Blang* is only a name. 'It is not functional at all', said community facilitator Muhammad Ridha. In 2015, the Aceh-based civil society organisation PKPM interviewed hundreds of farmers, community figures and government officials in order to revitalise *Keujruen Blang*. The research aimed to highlight the importance of *Keujruen Blang*, and to depict the governance of *Keujruen Blang* in the existing Aceh agricultural system, its substantial typological knowledge, and its relevance to the dynamics of development and agriculture. PKPM closely collaborated with the local government, the Indigenous Community Council or *Majelis Masyarakat Adat* (MAA), and the local agricultural agency to socialise their research findings and explore the potential for cooperation. This was to follow up and implement the recommendations from the research.

One of the reasons *Keujruen Blang* had weakened was the establishment of the Water User Farmer Association or *Perkumpulan Petani Pemakai Air* (P3A), an organisation created by the government with a similar role to that of *Keujruen Blang*. In 1997, the Aceh Besar district established 176 P3As. However, these P3As are not working optimally in managing rice fields, and have failed to replace the function of *Keujruen Blang*. *Keujruen Blang* functioned not only as the agricultural leader, but also as a mediator if there was conflict among farmers. P3A is less effective because it ignores existing values in the community. For example, most of its management members are directly appointed without involving farmers, and as a result, it has failed to gain the support of the people. 'P3A is not rooted in society', said

Ridha. The community is also often confused when differentiating between *Keujruen Blang* and P3A. In several areas of Aceh Besar, P3A is seen as replacing *Keujruen Blang*. In other areas, the *Keujruen Blang* still exists, but with a narrower role – only managing rice field water traditionally.

In yet other areas, however, *Keujreun Blang* is becoming increasingly relevant. In addition to serving as social capital to bring the community together, this indigenous institution is a facility to strengthen democracy at the grassroots level. It also has the potential to create food security and improve the welfare of farmers.

PKPM saw that an opportunity to revitalise the role of *Keujruen Blang* is significant in the context of the new Village Law (Law 6/2014). This law acknowledges local institutions within society. The Aceh government has also made a regulation in this matter. Most recently, the Aceh governor released Regulation Number 45/2015 on '*Keujruen Blang* Irrigation Management'. In this regulation the term P3A is eliminated. 'Now there is a strong sense of acknowledgement of local and indigenous wisdom', the PKPM organiser Ridha said. However, this regulation has not been followed up with the necessary technical measures. 'There is yet to be a real strategy from the district government', Ridha continued.

PKPM found that the community and government officials at the grassroots level hope that *Keujruen Blang* can be revitalised. This issue arose because, in addition to rice fields being under-managed, farmers did not want to fight over water for their land. Even though the conflicts remain small, these frictions disrupt relationships between the people. 'The community's wish should be responded accordingly by the local government', said Ridha. The Vice District Head of Aceh Besar, Syamsulrizal, is ready to cooperate with various parties to revitalise *Keujruen Blang* and said he has a strategy to make it happen. He will embrace members of the old *Keujruen Blang* and respected people in society. He will also hand over the election of the management to the farmers, as a campaign promise for his re-election.

Case study 8: Blessings from *mawah* – Foundation for People's Welfare (YKU), Aceh Besar

Min, the *keuchik* (village head), began by keeping one of his neighbour's cows. He is now a cattle boss in his hometown and owns 40 cows, having been in business since he was in senior high school in Banda Aceh in 1990. The number of the *keuchik's* cows increases every year, as there is always a cow giving birth. In 2015, there were 12 calves. The *keuchik* delivers some of his cows to his neighbours to be taken care of. In return, Min takes care of a number of cows belonging to the neighbours. This traditional financing and investment mechanism is called *mawah*, and does not only have economic benefits. 'It is effective in maintaining good relationships with neighbours', *Keuchik* Min said.

Mawah is a form or pattern of economic and business cooperation practised by the Acehnese, using a profit sharing system according to an initial agreement. This system is often applied in agriculture and on farms. For example, for cattle *mawah*, the profit sharing takes operational costs into consideration and the selling price of the cattle is calculated by the time spent raising it.

The Lamteuba people sell cows when they need school fees for their children. When the cow sold belongs to a neighbour, the profit will be evenly distributed between the owner and the caretaker. The local people depend on agriculture and livestock for their livelihood. 'This is an economic practice that is very helpful for the people', said Min, who is now providing capital to the *mawah* system.

Mawah became an alternative solution for poor people who had difficulty accessing capital through micro-credit programmes, due to their inability to meet the administrative provisions of micro-credit. Some did not have assets to serve as collateral, while others did not have a regular income to make the repayments. The *mawah* process begins with trust. Its success is highly dependent on the honesty of the beneficiaries.

There are three stages in *mawah*. First is a verbal agreement or handover in accordance with local customs. In Saree village, *mawah* practice is so common that they communicate via text messaging. The second stage is in regard to management and the third stage concerns sales and profit sharing. Currently, the profit sharing system is 70 per cent for the *mawah* receiver and 30 per cent for the capital provider.

Most people use their *mawah* practice as savings. In Saree for example, the youth use the profits from *mawah* to cover their future marriage costs. In Pidie, mothers created *mawah tiram* (savings) for 'just in case' purposes when their husbands were unable to set sail due to bad weather. '*Mawah* can also be an investment opportunity for external capital providers, to maintain good relationships between communities, and to strengthen food security', said Min.

During the past few years, the Aceh-based organisation YKU has worked with local NGOs and government officials to develop technical guidelines for *mawah* and a *syariah* index. The knowledge system's existence was threatened because many people possessing the knowledge were lost in the tsunami of 2004. YKU is presently developing operational guidelines to implement the *mawah* system in Aceh Besar.

The *Beng Mawah* Micro-Finance Institution was formed in Aceh Besar in 2012. Founded by a number of civil society organisation activists (including YKU), this institution provides capital access for its members in the fields of agriculture, farming and home industries. The loan is given without collateral, using a profit-sharing system. The receiver will gain 70 per cent profit, while the remainder goes to the *Beng Mawah* Micro-Finance Institution. This institution created a more modern *mawah* system. In this programme, besides presenting knowledge on improving the household economy through the *mawah* system, YKU has successfully established cooperation with key actors, both domestically and internationally, who have delved into this issue. Official cooperation includes memoranda of understanding between the Islamic Business and Economic Faculty of the Banda Aceh-based Islamic State University (UIN) and the local environmental NGO Yayasan Aceh Hijau. *Mawah* has also been adopted by the Regional Development Planning Agency (Bappeda).

Case study 9: Zero compromise in Torong Besi – Centre for Politics and Government, Gadjah Mada University (POLGOV UGM)

The Association of Indigenous People in Torong Besi, Manggarai district, on the island of Flores in East Nusa Tenggara, has become a symbol of the community's rejection of the exploitation of manganese ore in the area. Formed in 2007, the association is the hub of the Forest Circle Society Network that actively rejects the mining project because it destroys agricultural land and diminishes the community's ownership of its productive asset. This is in an area where no fewer than 75 per cent of households earn their livelihood as farmers and fishers.

Since 2013 there have been no mining activities. However, through this association, the local people remain vigilant about the possible return of miners. 'Our stand is clear, refusing all mining activities', said Simon Suban Tukan, one of the local figures in Torong Besi. The local people also built a cooperative enterprise to empower the local economy, so that they do not depend on foreign investment, particularly from the mining sector. Through the cooperative, the people cultivated pigs and cattle. Each community member voluntarily donates between Rp 50,000 and Rp 100,000 (US$4 to US$8) per month for the cooperative's business capital. By using a savings-and-loan system, the capital is often used to help local fishers.

This is a snapshot of how local people came up with an initiative to voice their rejection, starting by forming an association, then requesting advocacy support from environmental organisations and establishing a cooperative to build economic independence. They have a noble cause: early prevention of mining in protected forest areas. The local initiative described below is an effort by indigenous people to refuse mining projects in their area, which could be an example to other areas.

The Centre for Politics and Government at Gadjah Mada University (POLGOV UGM) has been documenting and supporting this local resistance to mining for the past few years. POLGOV and other civil society organisations engaged religious leaders to influence the policy-making process in Manggarai. POLGOV also supported the affected communities to work with several national NGO networks.

Mining exploitation in Torong Besi began in 1994 with the entry of companies such as PT. Arumbai and Istindo Mitra Oerdan (Colbran, 2010). Torong Besi is well known for producing manganese and its reserve at that time reached millions of tons. The problem was that the mining activity was located within a protected forest area, which was traditionally owned by the customary villages of Gendang Loce and Gendang Kerkuak. After PT Sumber Jaya Asia began operating in the area and massively mined manganese ore in early 2007, people started to see negative impacts. The manganese mining devastated the fishers' means of livelihood, as it polluted the beaches. Mining activities also clogged a number of water springs in the area, causing drought. The people were beginning to suffer from liver disease due to breathing manganese dust. By early 2008, there were at least three local people who had died because of this illness. 'There is no longer comfort here, only anger', said Yakobus Daud, an indigenous figure in Robek village, describing the situation at the time.

No longer able to stand the increasing impacts of mining, in early 2008 a number of indigenous figures gathered the people of Torong Besi. They agreed to go to the local government office and the Manggarai Local People's Representative to complain. Their visit was completely ignored. This happened a few times. 'We demanded the mining companies in our area be shut down', said Gaspar Sales, the head of the Gincu Indigenous *kampung* in Robek village.

They finally changed their strategy by requesting support from well-known national civil society networks, including the Alliance for Indigenous People (AMAN), the Indonesian Forum for the Environment (WALHI), and the Mining Advocacy Network (JATAM).

The composition of local actors varies. In Manggarai, with its Christian culture, the church plays a significant role in revitalising local knowledge on ecological preservation in the context of religious norms. The church is active in facilitating political processes that consolidate collective actions by indigenous communities around mines. It also establishes strategic alliances and coalitions with AMAN, WALHI and JATAM. Under the Ruteng diocese, this advocacy network is connected locally, nationally and globally.

With this support, local communities were able to develop better advocacy skills. In addition to demonstrations, the network prepared various advocacy strategies, from opinion forming in mass media to class action suits. For example, Simon Suban Tukan, a well-known former member of the provincial House of Representatives in East Nusa Tenggara, helped with advocacy efforts at the provincial and district government level.

This resistance finally showed results. The Manggarai District Government ceased the mining activities of PT Sumber Jaya Asia in Torong Besi. Strong pressure from the people drove the head of the Manggarai district, Christian Rotok, to revoke the company's business licence in 2009. The district head also regulated a cessation of all exploitation activities in the protected forest area of Torong Besi. Since then, the people of Torong Besi have been committed to never compromising on any mining activities, especially in protected forests. The people of Torong Besi optimised communal and indigenous ownership principles as pressure to influence policy.

Case study 10: Traditional insurance – *Lembaga Advokasi HIV/AIDS (LAHA)* Institute for HIV/AIDS Advocacy, Kendari

In Konawe Selatan (Southeast Sulawesi), the spirit of sharing does not know the meaning of loss. They call this *melesi*, which means sharing the burden or lightening each other's load in times of happiness or grief. *Melesi* is taken from the language of the Tolaki, the ethnic group in Konawe Selatan. Assistance is given when there is misfortune (such as death), or for the school fees of a neighbour going to school outside of the area, or for a marriage. 'We generally come bringing money or coconuts', said Haryanto Yunus, a community organiser.

According to Haryanto, the *melesi* tradition comes from the spirit of togetherness and mutual assistance. This tradition is intrinsic in the social lives of the local community and has been preserved for generations. Based on this idea, a number of community groups wanted to institutionalise *melesi* as a formal policy. One of its concrete forms is the translation of *melesi* into a self-funded community health insurance scheme.

In August 2015, LAHA held focus group discussions in four villages of Ranomeeto Barat sub-district, Southeast Sulawesi, on the integration of *melesi* as a complementary element to formal health insurance. The committee asked participants about their experience in using the local community health insurance.[12] For example, did they still have to pay fees outside the ones covered by the health insurance scheme?

The results showed that almost all the participants paid additional fees above the insurance coverage. They still used *melesi* when a neighbour was experiencing misfortune. Therefore, they conveyed the idea that *melesi* should be integrated into the local health insurance system of Southeast Sulawesi and linked with the Social Security Implementing Agency or *Badan Penyelenggara Jaminan Sosial (BPJS)*. 'We want *melesi* to have a legal basis', said Haryanto.

The process to formalise *melesi* did not go smoothly at the beginning, with some community groups rejecting the idea. They suspected this activity was only to raise funds for personal interest. Socialisation was then intensified in a number of locations, convincing the communities of the importance of active participation in providing health insurance. Haryanto explained that they needed to guarantee that *melesi* would benefit them in times of grief.

After some time, this process began to run relatively smoothly, and this was aided in September 2016 by a decision for all departments of government to sign an agreement to support *melesi*-based village

[12] Wanting community-managed health insurance can be seen as a reaction to operational problems (for example, the strict referral system and slow process) of the national and sub-national government universal health insurance schemes (BPJS Kesehatan and Jamkesda) that were introduced in the mid-2000s after decentralisation and direct election of sub-national leaders. Popular health schemes led to success at the polls and became an electoral asset during the election. See Pisani et al, 2016, for further discussion on the political journey of Indonesia's universal health coverage programme.

health insurance. 'The key is the guarantee that *melesi* is equipped with a supervisory body elected by the people', said Haryanto.

The government also regulated the premiums for *melesi*. The premium to be paid by heads of families is determined by community agreement. The only thing differentiating *melesi* from formal insurance is the benefit paid. Under formal insurance, the government or insurance provider determines the amount of benefit paid, but under *melesi*, Haryanto says, the people establish the amount, 'depending on the result of village discussions'.

Haryanto thinks *melesi* can also bring other benefits to villages. For example, if in a specific time period the insurance coverage is not used by *melesi* members, it can be turned into deposits. If unused, this fund can be used to develop village-owned enterprises. These enterprises would then distribute the profits from productive activities in the village. '*Melesi* teaches independence and active participation in village development processes', said Haryanto.

Since October 2015, with the help of LAHA, a number of villages have started to develop a draft of the '*Melesi* Local Culture Village Regulation'. One of the resource people invited for this drafting was the head of the Law and Legislation Section of the South Konawe Selatan government, Risman Kudaso. After the draft is complete, the village leadership socialises it and establishes a managing agency in each village.

Risman encouraged every village to develop village regulations to formalise *melesi*. 'That way other villages can replicate this', said Risman. In the discussion, a number of indigenous institutions expect the local government to provide support in the form of stimulus for initial financing. According to Haryanto, one of the challenges to implementing *melesi*-based insurance is fund management capacity. In his opinion, village officials still need support for a period of time. 'That is why support from the government and village figures is crucial', he said.

Risman Kudaso said that *melesi* is a translation of the Local Regulation Number 22/2013 on *Mandara Mendidoha Desa* (Healthy and Smart Village). According to him, this regulation can serve as a legal umbrella for the implementation of *melesi* village health insurance. He noted that *melesi* has just been implemented in Ranomeeto Barat sub-district, and more and more villages are implementing it.

FIVE

Generating and managing local knowledge

The next two chapters will discuss how knowledge is generated, managed and used in real time, by real actors, in real political contexts. We build on reports that the ten grantees produced for the KSI project, many extracts from which are presented here in the ensuing text. Chapter Five focuses on the generation, codification and management of local knowledge, while Chapter Six focuses on the use and uptake of local knowledge by policy makers.

Generating local knowledge

Citizens and organisations have different positions and roles in producing local knowledge: to solve a local problem; to recommend alternatives for solving problems; to anticipate potential problems; or to preserve local wisdom. These different roles are defined by different capacities of organisations to understand local issues and know the local political context, including related stakeholders.

The *melesi* community-managed health insurance system in Konawe Selatan, Southeast Sulawesi, for example, reflects a continuity of communal solidarity with improvements in financial governance that address emerging health problems. This is part of an effort to contribute to a growing government-sponsored universal health coverage system. This system is possible and sustainable because it is built on the 'past', that is, on the community's social capital and local wisdom, along with the development of a 'modern' health insurance scheme. Local systems are built on or aligned with existing belief systems, which is not a totally new thing. It is not like creating a new institution. In this case, the basis for a local health financing strategy is the existing values of traditional mutual assistance (*melesi*) instead of 'rational technical-based' health financing solutions:

> The creation of village health insurance in Konawe Selatan is achieved by adopting *melesi*, where each head of a family routinely pays a mandatory premium to the managing agency established by the village government. The amount of the premium is set based on the result of village community discussions, not based on risk. *Melesi* is part of a local cultural heritage from the values of unity and helping each other, or *samaturu medulu ronga mepokoo aso*. The creation of this communal health insurance demonstrates an implementation of such values. In addition, the *melesi* village health insurance scheme can be a basis on which to build village-owned enterprises. It might also serve as a village micro-finance institution to help people gain access to capital in developing productive businesses in the village. This *melesi* village health insurance scheme is a model that can be implemented by the villagers due to their values of collaboration and solidarity, access to high-cost referral health service facilities, and large economic gaps in the village. This *melesi* village insurance scheme will also teach independence and active community participation in the village development process. (LAHA)

Local knowledge is embedded in practice, action, morality and spirituality; it has a central role in social relations and reciprocity among people, as well as in the unity of people and nature. *Keujruen*

Blang, water distribution through an irrigation system in Aceh Besar, serves as a communal mechanism for water distribution as well as a venue for broader conflict resolution among community members. It is a proven and effective communal platform that is rooted in the cultural structure of the community. It provides culturally legitimate conflict resolution (as opposed to legal-formal mechanisms provided by the government-managed irrigation committee). As reported by PKPM Aceh, by the end of the 1990s the government had established 176 farmer organisations (P3A) to manage irrigation systems, a legal and formal mechanism. The intention of P3A was to 'modernise' the management of irrigation systems at the community level. However, in Aceh Besar, only a few are still functioning, leading to conflict between farmers. At the same time, water-associated disputes among farmers in areas where *Keujruen Blang* is in place are mostly resolved locally and without conflict.

> People in Aceh possess knowledge that has been practised for generations on arranging and managing rice fields. This knowledge forms the characteristics of rice field system management by the Acehnese. The existence of the traditional institution of *Keujruen Blang* as local wisdom is very important, because most Acehnese make their living as farmers, and the biggest contribution to the local economy comes from the agriculture sector. *Keujruen Blang* plays an important role in managing rice field agricultural governance and systems. This includes not only managing irrigation and water distribution, leading to the implementation of various traditional and community work activities, and making mutual agreements among farmers; it also responds to critical issues that are difficult to address, such as resolving conflicts among rice farmers. These roles have very strong relevance to sustainable agricultural development and the broader socio-economic development agenda, as *Keujruen Blang* principles and practices can strengthen social capital and local democratisation, support food security,

create harmony and peace, and ultimately improve the welfare of farmers. (PKPM Aceh)

Interaction and adaption with the local environment

We have argued that there are close interactions between local knowledge and the physical environment. Our case studies share a common understanding of local knowledge in communities as a product of co-evolution between communities and their environments. This co-evolution serves as a foundation for and result of local community livelihoods and cultures. Local knowledge, such as the clan-based water management system in Kupang (East Nusa Tenggara) documented by Pikul, showcases the interdependence of socio-economic and ecological spheres. This interdependence explains why traditional water management in Kupang has been more effective and functional than the external technocratic mechanism installed through the government's community water and sanitation infrastructure project, PAMSIMAS (see case study 1 on page 60).

PUSKA UI's science field shop is also a place where interdisciplinary and trans-disciplinary knowledge, dialogue and exchange can take place. In this arena, farmers, anthropologists, agro-meteorologists and students from different disciplinary backgrounds learn from each other and engage in discussion on the vulnerabilities caused by climate change. Together, they formulate possible adaptation strategies. Despite learning about scientific methods, farmers have not abandoned traditional knowledge systems. Farmers still refer to several things that they have known for a long time to predict the planting season. 'The existence of cicadas signifies the dry season, while the appearance of bamboo sprouts can be an indication of the rainy season', a PUSKA UI community facilitator said. 'The combination of traditional, empirical and scientific methods has helped farmers address the agricultural impacts of climate change', he continued. Farmers still routinely gather every month to discuss agro-meteorology and consider this an important learning process.

In some of our cases, local knowledge and its related local institutions are also challenged by rapid socio-economic and environmental changes. Shocks and trends can lead to dramatic losses of local knowledge, as during the 2004 tsunami in Aceh.

> In Aceh, conflicts and the tsunami have destroyed natural resources (rice fields, plantations, fish ponds, salt ponds, livestock and plants) and physical resources (public infrastructure). They have weakened human resources (deceased, lost, missed educational opportunities, sickness/injury) and crushed social resources (trust, social harmony, the culture of helping each other, caring for one another, the spirit of cooperation). (PKPM Aceh)

The challenge is to assess what remains the same (or survives) amid the rapid changes taking place in many communities. *Sasi,* the community-based natural resource management on the island of Haruku, Central Maluku, illustrates the point. *Sasi* is recognition of the role of communities in managing and maintaining landscape mosaics and biodiversity. Under *sasi* principles, fishing is not just a livelihood activity but also a mix of cultural and environmental matters. *Sasi* is well accepted and environmentally friendly because it assures a culturally fair distribution of the resources among community members. Fishing activities are guided by conservation principles. *Sasi* contributes to promoting sustainable economic and social conditions in the fishing sector because the mechanism makes fishing operations as selective as possible; it retains target specimens of the right species and size, with minimum impact on other species or juvenile fish of the target species. This practice is also 'community-friendly', as it helps maintain the necessary environmental balance for stable and predictable economic activity. Nevertheless, *sasi* is dynamic and adapting to a changing environment:

> The sasi principle is: 'For everything, there is a season.' The sasi practice is an idea from indigenous people intended to preserve

the sustainability of life by restricting resource exploitation and forbidding harvest before harvest time. For example, if a coconut is prematurely picked, while economically valuable, it will not produce a new coconut. Likewise, mining sand and stone will reduce the quality of coastal sea water.

The local community in the village seemed to have lost the ability to weave and develop customs and norms that are meant to be the basis of their collective behaviour. This is due to them having been disconnected from their cultural roots. Justice in natural resource management is not fulfilled because the local community does not have access to participate in all the stages of management. Striving to preserve natural resources will be even harder if licences are given to businesses dredging resources without considering the preservation and existence of 'sasi' as a local culture worthy of being maintained. (PATTIRO)

In many cases, traditional knowledge was destroyed by modernisation.

There is now very limited traditional natural resource management on the island of Timor, as the resources to be managed are either no longer there or have changed due to various development or extractive projects, not necessarily agreed by the local community. Therefore, local knowledge on the planting season, harvest season, community granary and natural protection could no longer be applied; the role of the traditional leader is no longer acknowledged. The role of traditional elders in natural resource management was significant. They would conduct ceremonies to open land, decide on planting and harvest time, collect harvest as food reserves, and establish restrictions on hunting and collecting forest products during certain times. However, with the establishment of uniform village governance with Law 5/1979, this role was no longer recognised. Gradually, only a few villages were still using local knowledge and acknowledging local institutions in preserving nature and managing natural resource use. (Pikul)

Interaction between forms of knowledge

In Chapter Two, we emphasised the importance of the complementary nature of various knowledge systems, and the need to move away from translating knowledge into one currency. A case of climate adaptation among farmers in Indramayu, West Java, demonstrates the complementary nature of local knowledge. Scientists from the University of Indonesia worked together with local farmers to understand the climate and its impact on agricultural activities. PUSKA UI's study suggests that we need to propose a 'multiple-evidence approach' instead of using the single 'knowledge currency' of formal science. Indigenous, local and scientific knowledge systems generate equally valid, complementary and useful evidence for interpreting conditions, change trajectories and in some cases causal relationships relevant to the sustainable governance of ecosystems and biodiversity (Tengö et al, 2014). Our case studies confirm that a multiple-evidence approach requires greater participation of local communities, as highlighted below.

> Since 2009, the Indramayu Farmers Club, facilitated by PUSKA UI, has learned agro-meteorology in science field shops. Several farmer groups, local NGOs and agro-meteorology experts from Indonesia, the Netherlands and Africa have collaborated through this programme. Beginning with an acknowledgement from local farmers that their traditional weather forecasting system had been misleading in recent years, they learned to monitor and calculate rainfall, combine scientific methods with monitoring rice field conditions, animal behaviour, pests and plant diseases that they routinely record. 'This monitoring results in planting period estimations,' said Yusup, a member of the Indramayu Rainfall Observation Club. Farmers are developing a new behaviour: they have become researchers. Farmers who previously carried hoes now also carry pens and books. (PUSKA UI)

On the island of Timor, Pikul brought local knowledge around water management to the attention of the academic community as it generated solid information on local water management. A local university, Artha Wacana Christian University (*Universitas Kristen Artha Wacana*), noted that the research findings influenced the policies of the Masehi Injili Church in Timor, one of the largest protestant churches in eastern Indonesia.

> In communicating with policy makers, support from the scientific community is a requirement that cannot be ignored. Support from universities and scientists goes hand in hand with the empowerment objective by civil society, so that local knowledge receives scientific legitimacy and its methods are held accountable. More importantly, with support from the academic/scientific community, local knowledge can be heard by policy makers whose institutional knowledge is still in the classical/conventional paradigm. Based on Pikul's experience, the scientific community is somewhat inspired by local knowledge to develop new knowledge to effectively resolve issues. The scientific community has also contributed significantly to developing and refining the local knowledge development methodology. Moreover, a number of international policies (such as the Convention on Biological Diversity, and the United Nations Framework Convention on Climate Change) have promoted the adoption of local knowledge in their implementation. This has strengthened various lessons learned on developing local knowledge in a way that is communicable with policy makers. (Pikul)

Several partners incorporated religious beliefs into their advocacy. A good example of this is LK3, a civil society organisation based in Banjarmasin. One of its focuses is the promotion of traditional knowledge to strengthen the understanding of Islam among the people. This idea is elaborated by LK3 through a number of activities, such as monitoring and advocacy of community development projects, and environmental awareness programmes. In implementing these activities, LK3 collaborates with other institutions, such as the Jakarta-based Wahid Institute on the issues of democracy, pluralism, women and local culture. The film, 'Our River, Our Life' is one of the outputs of the LK3 programme focusing on revitalising river culture in the face of climate change, in which river management is indicative of the close relationship between local wisdom, religion, everyday life and the physical environment.

> The river, in the context of Banjar, contains many stories. These stories are about the struggles, ideas and behaviours of the Banjar people in interpreting the river as their source of life. From the process of dialogue and activities related to river revitalisation advocacy, LK3 found a number of stories very closely related to the relationship between people and the river. One is the story of Khaidir Prophet as the protector of the river. As told by a cultural observer in Banjarmasin, the story says:
>
>> In the beliefs of the Banjar people, a number of prophets have been watching over the river. That is why when we go to the river, we are asked to send greetings and prayers, and act politely and kindly to the river, because the river will show its fury when treated poorly. The one who is protecting the river until now is believed to be Khaidir Prophet. The river will give its best prayers to people who treat it nicely, and vice versa.
>
> Another similar story is that the river has prayer beads and will pray for anyone who is friendly towards it. Among signs of God's greatness, there are verses known as *kauniyah*, namely verses on invisible things. The environment, including the river with all of its content, is included in *kauniyah* verses as proof of God's greatness. (LK3)

In these folk tales, we see that the river is very meaningful for the community around Banjarmasin. While the tales could be viewed as nothing more than myths, they reflect a form of local wisdom around preserving balance and harmony between humans and their environment, a cognitive map for adapting to the environment. These stories are generated from the Banjar people's long struggle responding to changes in nature and their surroundings. The stories are rarely heard anymore and exist only in stories told by the elders who once lived peacefully with the river. As the population grows and development rapidly expands, and the number of outsiders visiting increases, these narratives are heard less and less. Appreciating these stories is another form of appreciating local knowledge.

Locality and origin

At the community level, the challenge faced is, 'How local is local knowledge?' Some elements in local knowledge are truly local and some are adopted/adapted from outside the community. Our cases identify both unique and common dimensions of local knowledge. On the one hand, partners have compiled various forms of local knowledge that are not only unique to every culture or society in the study, but also demonstrate variation within communities. On the other hand, the findings share some similarities and patterns. Looking across our ten cases, we can find a pattern: even knowledge that is seen as locally specific is similar in principle and practice to knowledge in other locations, even in locations with significantly different socio-cultural backgrounds. For example, research by the Indonesian Institute of Sciences (LIPI) (Cahyadi, 2012) and others (Von Benda-Beckmann et al, 1992; Nikijuluw, 1998) show practices similar to *sasi* outside the Maluku islands, revealing that the principles of indigenous coastal fisheries management in *sasi* are also found in other locations, such as Sulawesi and Papua. *Mawah* – the community-based asset and profit sharing mechanism in Aceh – and the *melesi* community health scheme in Southeast Sulawesi share principles of *gotong royong* (customary mutual assistance) that are also widely found in other parts of Indonesia with different socio-economic backgrounds. These all lead us to the question of what it means to be 'local' and how we set boundaries in terms of place and location of local knowledge.

Only one of our cases (*sasi* in Maluku) reported an estimation of when the practice was initiated (in the 1600s). The other studies have no specific information on the origin of local knowledge. In general, they mention that the knowledge and practices were inherited from their ancestors, and passed down from generation to generation. Like other non-tangible artefacts, such as vernacular knowledge and practices, verification of their genesis and origin in terms of time and source of practice is difficult, if not impossible, to ascertain. This might have something to do with the prominence of oral culture in Indonesia (Heryanto, 2015) in which it is difficult to track the lineage of knowledge.

Another dimension that makes the genesis and originality of local knowledge even more complex is the fact that local knowledge – as are all types of knowledge – is dynamic as it adapts to a changing environment. Because local knowledge changes over time, it can be difficult to trace where it came from, and when, to know which actors engaged in the local knowledge process, and even to decide whether a practice or local knowledge system is local, adopted from outside, or a blend of local and introduced components. In most of the cases reported by partners the latter situation is likely.

> For a very long time, the Aceh people have developed and practised *mawah* in rural areas as a coping strategy to gain access to capital. The *mawah* practice is based on social capital (familial relationship, care for each other, spirit of helping each other, trust), which then facilitates access to financial or resource capital. In the economic context, *mawah* brings together parties with surplus assets but limited labour and time, and parties with limited assets but surplus labour. *Mawah* combines two important factors in production activity: owners of working capital ('*ureung po atra*') and labour ('*ureung keurija*'/'*pubuet*' or '*pemawah*'). In *mawah* cooperation, *pemawah* usually contributes to work

supporting facilities, such as farming tools for agricultural *mawah* or barns for livestock *mawah*. The vulnerability factors discussed previously demanded that people adopt new means of livelihood generation or modified their previous livelihood approaches. They also decreased the chances of people engaging in 'traditional' *mawah* for agriculture, plantation and livestock. The concept of *mawah* as a traditional coping strategy in rural areas is being reapplied for new livelihoods, and even in urban areas. People are starting to implement the *mawah* concept in their modern business practices, such as managing property or businesses, including cafés, shops and car and motorcycle washes. In these cooperative enterprises, the capital owner and the manager mutually agree on the profit and loss sharing of the business, just like in the traditional *mawah*. Under the modern *mawah*, people in cities have begun to use written agreements, or even a notary. (YKU)

The fact that local knowledge is described as being based on people's daily life experiences means that local knowledge is attached to the physical places where people live, work and act. Therefore, there are inherent barriers to external actors documenting and translating local knowledge. According to Relph (1976: 45), places have identities and meanings for the people who live there. 'The identity of a place is an expression of the adaptation of assimilation, accommodation and the socialisation of knowledge to each other.' With this understanding, the concept of place means different things to different people depending on their personal relationship to it. External researchers may present 'inauthentic attitudes to place', which do not involve understanding a place or its symbolic meanings, identity and values due to their 'outsideness' (Seamon and Sowers, 2008) as well as their efforts to comply with a research methodology that requires 'objective attitudes'. Places are instead seen as backgrounds for action, situations and environments where research activities are situated. While politicians and decision makers often regard places this way (a place is geographic coordinates, figures, data – called an 'objective outsideness attitude' by

Seamon and Sowers, 2008: 45), local knowledge researchers who want to document and translate local knowledge need to deeply understand meanings, values and identities associated with physical place. They need to experience behavioural 'insideness' as an objective observer (known as an 'emic approach' within anthropology). Researchers who have deeper connections with local people may become empathetic which demands 'willingness to be open to significances of a place, to feel it, to know and respect its symbols' (Relph, 1976: 54). In this way, researchers can begin to overcome the limitations imposed by being outsiders.

There might be a need to be innovative in the efforts to document local wisdom so that it can contribute to the policy making process. The BIGS story about forest management in Central Java is a good example. BIGS innovated by visualising its research outcome in an animated film, which was then shown to villagers. Disseminating ideas through this film provided the opportunity for the villagers to respond, both critiquing and praising the video. It also brought out new and other ideas based on and related to the animation. The villagers' response was useful not only as an external validation to the research result, but also as material to develop policies. New ideas and other stories concerning culture-based forest conservation conveyed by the villagers are actually very rich in establishing policy options for environmental conservation based on local knowledge, as shown in the graph in Figure 5.1.

LOCAL KNOWLEDGE MATTERS

Figure 5.1: BIGS innovation for local knowledge

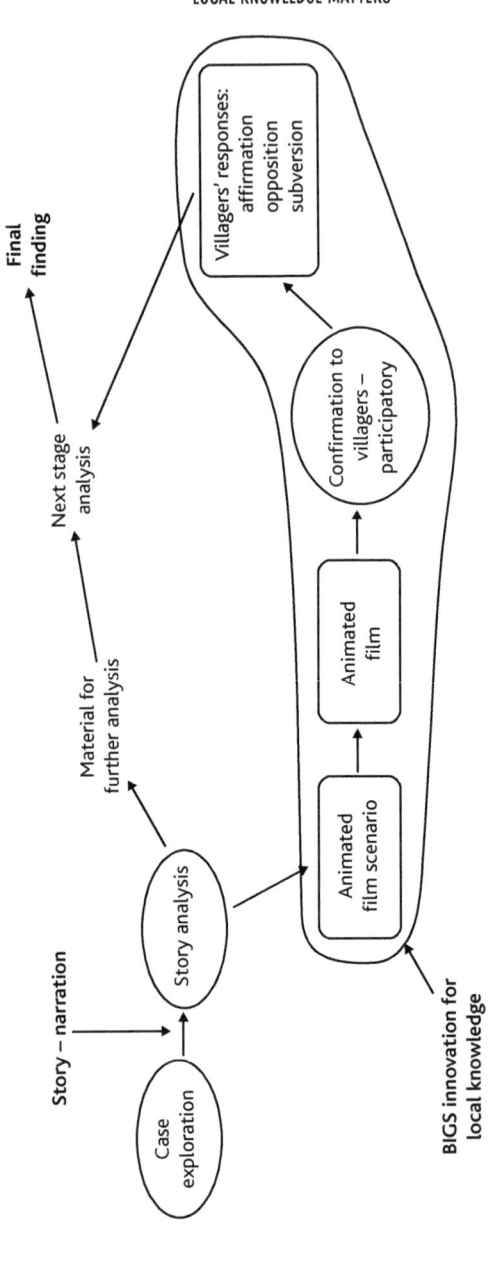

The political economy of generating and managing local knowledge

It is not sufficient to simply document local knowledge; it is equally important to understand how this knowledge adapts, develops and changes over time, how it contributes to equality or inequality, how inclusive it is, who benefits from holding local knowledge and who loses by being left out. In addition, in terms of local knowledge-to-policy processes, how this knowledge is communicated and by whom, both within and beyond the community, is also significant. These are the social complexities of local knowledge. From a critical perspective, as local knowledge resides, grows and is owned through socio-economic relations, its 'fairness' from critical theory and social inclusion perspectives can be questioned. By and large, local knowledge documented in our studies is owned by the elites in a place. The framework developed by FAO (FAO, 2004), which we mentioned in Chapter Two, is a useful starting point to navigate the data across our case studies: *common knowledge* is held by most people in a community; *shared knowledge* is held by many but not all community members as part of a division of labour and roles; and *specialised knowledge* is held by a those with special training or authority. Using this framework, 'specialised knowledge' is held by a few people who might have held a special position (for example, the clan that controls the water system in Kupang), or as 'common/shared knowledge' that is held by many but not all community members (for example, villagers in Aceh who raise livestock will know more about basic animal husbandry and the *mawah* system than those without livestock). Only two studies (the community-based health insurance system in Sulawesi and forest conservation in Central Java) identified local knowledge as 'common knowledge' that is held by most people in a community. The POLGOV study of local resistance to mining showed the mixed use of specialised knowledge and common knowledge: specialised knowledge of religious issues (church and mosque), environmental advocacy (NGOs) and the local community merged in the resistance movement against mining projects.

The power of inequity within local knowledge has significant implications for research and development work (FAO, 2004). To find out what people know, the political-economy position and the right people must be identified, because possessing knowledge is a consequence of people's political economy position. This requires deep understanding of the socio-economic arrangement of the community; in some cases, this is concealed by formal structures and traditions. We sometimes draw the wrong conclusion if we work with the wrong informants – because the sampling follows the formal structure or works within a given framework. An analysis of local knowledge, identifying who owns it and how they actualise and communicate it, is not a simple task; it requires an adequate stock of knowledge about the structure of both formal and informal knowledge systems behind the proxies for local knowledge. For example, if in Aceh Besar young men do the herding, they may know better than their fathers and the owner of the cows where the best grazing sites are, so asking fathers to show good pastures (because a researcher would normally go to the elders first) might only provide partial information. Selecting the head of the household (the fathers) as the informant is an example of taking facts at face value, because it follows the conventional household structure. This approach to knowledge is related to the belief system about the role of the head of the household in an agriculture-based community and in intra-household power relations in Aceh. Political-economic inquiries will not only see this from the perspective of specialisation or an age-based division of labour in the community, but from a broader (political) understanding of the knowledge system and where specific knowledge resides.

Local knowledge is not equally shared and owned by men and women, between age groups, ordinary men and ordinary people, among other variations. Each of these social categories may possess different and complementary knowledge. Many cases, such as the clan-based water management system in Kupang, whale hunting in Lembata and *sasi* fishery management in Maluku show that culturally designated individuals, lineages or clans may possess specialised knowledge and skills in specific domains. The story from Aceh Besar on revitalising customary farmers' associations is one example.

> Women play an extremely important role in fulfilling the needs of farming families in Aceh Besar. Women farmers play a central and dominant role in rice field related activities, such as making seedbeds, sowing the seeds, applying fertilisers, removing seeds and planting rice. Women farmers are responsible for ensuring that water flows to the rice fields, and for preventing the water from spilling and disrupting the growth of the paddy, leaving it vulnerable to pest attack. To guarantee the availability of water, women stay up late at night to control water supply, because other farmers could close the waterway or there could be leakage in the irrigation, and the water would not reach the rice fields. Women also play a crucial role in mediating water distribution conflicts among farmers. (PKPM Aceh)

There are often roles for 'non-elite' community members such as women, children and minority groups in transmitting, preserving and elaborating local knowledge. For example, women are frequently the primary managers or collectors of natural resources, such as drinking water, or of fuel or small agro-forestry plots or medicinal plants. They are also the primary holders of knowledge concerning such resources. However, they are often not present in decision-making events on the distribution of these communal resources. Special care must therefore be taken to involve women and other under-represented groups.

> In implementing activities to revitalise river management in Banjarmasin, LK3 always engages women's groups, often even more than men's groups. Women's participation has been important in initiating several activities, such as proposing and coordinating social action to clean the river. LK3 realised that women are often more affected than men; thus it is very important to involve women in the public space and engage them in public policy-making processes. Men do not dominate

attendance at public discussions. During events, women are active in responding to resource people and in conveying issues from their neighbourhoods. At one event, the female participants came from various religious and social organisations in Banjarmasin city and at regional and city levels, such as Muslimat, Badan Kontak Majelis Taklim (BKMT) and Nasyiatul Aisiyah. Also included were other women's organisations, such as the Women's Organisation Coordination Agency, Indonesian Christian Women, Indonesian Catholic Women, Wandani, WHDI, Aisiyah and others. These organisations are part of LK3's network and they are always involved when LK3 hosts events. (LK3)

Access to knowledge is governed by culturally specific rules and procedures. Communities often see this kind of gender and social hierarchy-based division of labour not as a power relation issue, but as a cultural approach, indicating that women and men have different, but complementary, roles and responsibilities. Our studies acknowledge that this has resulted in different knowledge, needs, concerns, priorities and roles within communities. Attention to gender balance and social inclusion in all local knowledge processes is critical to understanding the knowledge itself and how it is used for policy purposes.

Methods and instruments to codify information and knowledge

Let us now turn to how our partners codified local knowledge. This is important because local knowledge – as all forms of knowledge – needs to be generated and codified in order to be become part of the knowledge sector. How this is done will affect how the knowledge is used. Using the FAO framework (Figure 5.1), the methods and instruments to collect local knowledge were different depending on the type of knowledge. For 'common knowledge' such as myths and communal traditions, the methods used were storytelling and key actors' analysis (the *mawah* system, *melesi*, myths in forest conservation and so on). For 'shared knowledge', the common method was observation of key events or processes. For example, in the *sasi* coastal fishery system in Maluku, PATTIRO observed the ritual and process, and did an analysis of the key actors involved in the events and their specific roles.

> Another challenge to implementing sasi is that many people think it is only mandatory for local people, and does not apply to 'outsiders' who are governed by formal (government) regulations. As a result, indigenous people and groups are striving for *sasi lompa* to be formally reinforced according to their ancestral heritage. 'The central Maluku government with the provincial government intend to draft, socialise and issue a local regulation on *sasi*. This is the opportunity for us to give inputs, so the Haruku King is involved,' said Haji Abdullah Latarissa, a local leader. The challenge being addressed is how tradition-based local knowledge can be codified so that multiple parties involved in the policy-making process can understand it. (PATTIRO)

This codification process is crucial to overcome discrepancies of understanding among community groups; the basic benefit of the *sasi lompa* codification is to strengthen social cohesion and preserve the fishery resources for community benefit. If the codification process is participatory, people can see whether their understanding is the same as other community members. This stage is important because local knowledge cannot be separated from the 'owner' of such knowledge. There are many actors who contribute to local knowledge and our cases show a large range of knowledge producers and users.

> *Religious institutions and civil society organisations*: In Manggarai, religious institutions redefined social norms and enriched them with religious norms, and contextualised them to be relevant to the current context. For example, the church mediated indigenous community networks around manganese

mines. Its goal was to revitalise and consolidate community knowledge and establish strategic alliances with various civil society organisations, such as AMAN, WALHI and JATAM. (POLGOV)

Civil society coalitions: There are on-going efforts by a coalition of civil society organisations in Banyuwangi to save the ecology of the Tumpang Pitu area from gold mining corporations. The coalition consists of Banyuwangi's Forum for Environmental Learning, or *Forum Peduli Masyarakat Nelayan Banyuwangi*, and *Front Nahdliyin untuk Kedaulatan Sumber Daya Alam*. (POLGOV)

Government and multi stakeholders: Our study engaged multiple partners, including local government (Bappeda, the Marine Affairs and Fisheries Office and the Environmental Agency), the local people's representative and indigenous people (including the Indigenous Council and Kewang), the fishers' association, and extractive companies operating in the Maluku Tengah district. (PATTIRO)

In terms of approach, in engaging local knowledge actors to gather data, a fundamental dichotomy can be observed across our ten cases. The first group used a process by which academic researchers and professional practitioners collaborate; the practitioners are either involved in the research or carry it out themselves with the support of professional researchers. Examples of this approach are in PUSKA UI on climate change adaptation research with farmers in Indramayu, and in POLGOV UGM with communities in Manggarai on land-dispute advocacy. The approach involved using 'research-minded' local knowledge actors in the data collection and analysis process.

> The process involves codification of local practices into a conceptual framework with three essential components: 1) conducting participatory research (research scientists and local

farmers); 2) conducting on-site oriented research (research scientists, extension workers and farmers); and 3) validating farmer experiments (farmers and extension workers). (PUSKA UI)

Through this perspective, the researchers carried out participatory on-station data collection and data validation, with the roles of the local knowledge actors limited to being informants. As such, this methodology may be perceived as hegemonic knowledge (Bergold and Thomas, 2012). The reason for this is that the research process starts from the external and is *about* the community (Russo, 2012).[1]

The second approach is found in a second, larger group of eight studies where the research was conducted directly with local knowledge holders. The aim was to reconstruct their knowledge and abilities in a process of understanding and empowerment. In these eight studies, research was conducted as research *with* the people in question, and about their problems. This approach was chosen because the aim of the inquiry and the research questions were not developed out of the convergence of two perspectives – that of science and of practice, but as research about the local knowledge and contextualisation of a given research question. What all other studies show is an effort to understand, communicate and empower local knowledge – an effort taken to address the nature of local knowledge that technically uses different forms of expression with other types of knowledge, especially scientific knowledge.

Mapping the distribution of local knowledge will enable us to analyse the sources of local knowledge that will lead to an analysis of power relations. Having a map of actors in the *mawah* system in Aceh Besar, for example, helped YKU to identify the land ownership structure and socio-economic structure of the society.

---

[1] Given their academic mandates, it should be little surprise that the two studies taking this perspective are university-based.

Globally, micro-finance has been the most popular approach to overcoming poverty in rural areas. This strategy has also been adopted by the government in Aceh as well as by multiple donor organisations during the post-tsunami rehabilitation and reconstruction period. It has contributed to the development of the micro-finance sector in Aceh over the last ten years. However, the socio-collateral approach used in micro-credit does not accommodate the context of the means of livelihood of the rural poor, who depend on the yields of agriculture, farms and sailing, with an unstable income and inability to regularly and routinely pay weekly or monthly instalments. These people do not own assets that can serve as collateral. The research found several cases in the study area where the inability of group members (generally the poor) to pay instalments has generated conflicts with other group members. This is because the 'punishment' over delinquency in payments affects the whole group – none of the group members will receive another loan, and the village will not receive funding for infrastructure development. As a result, the poor are ridiculed and are no longer involved in micro-finance activities. In some cases, poor people who have taken micro-credit from programmes funded by the government must take high-interest loans from loan sharks to pay the micro-credit instalments, because of their uneven and irregular income. Thus, instead of empowering, this programme is actually trapping poor people in a deeper cycle of debt and poverty. (YKU)

The socio-economic nature of local knowledge requires a context-specific data collection method and sampling approach that reflects the local socio-economic structure, as in the following case by POLGOV.

Knowledge has begun to be consolidated, structured and documented in a more organised way. Local knowledge has been transformed into explicit knowledge or common knowledge. Through an agenda-setting process, structured local knowledge can be promoted into an evidence base for public issues, public agendas and institutional agendas. Collective awareness and knowledge leads to discussions in public media, so the issues become public issues that can turn into policy issues when relevant parties in the policy process, especially formal actors, begin to view them as public concerns that need to be addressed. If such political agendas are accommodated and become part of the formal policy-making process, this will turn into a public agenda: a public issue generally recognised by the political community or policy makers as an agenda that needs to be considered and managed through relevant public authorities. (POLGOV)

Methods and instruments to manage information and knowledge

Once codified, knowledge needs to be managed. This allows organisations to use and adapt practices to leverage their existing knowledge assets and develop a culture of sharing and learning. In many cases, codified local knowledge lacks information about the socio-cultural context, a situation that puts local knowledge at the instrumental level. Bringing the everyday life of a community into broader conceptual debates requires an adequate stock of knowledge metadata: the 'who, what, where, when and how' of data collection.

In investigating the *mawah* system in Aceh Besar, for example, researchers reported difficulties in identifying the underlying socio-economic structures that made this mechanism function. This requires the researcher to have adequate knowledge about communal asset structures in Aceh Besar, the evolution of socio-economic class division in Aceh, and so on. In short, the challenge is about having an adequate relevant stock of knowledge so that the local knowledge can be understood. Multiple levels of community leaders in Acch are important figures in exploring local knowledge. They also function as intermediaries who can communicate local knowledge to the government.

As a result, when presented without the local and cultural context in which it was collected, local observations and knowledge can lose value at best, and be misleading at worst. For example, the community health insurance system documented by LAHA in Southeast Sulawesi was possible because of the cultural context of *melesi* – a community practice of shared poverty/property. *Melesi* is the context in which the health insurance system is situated. When LAHA was advocating for scaling up the insurance system, knowledge management issues constrained this effort. The data brought to district level as the basis for developing a district regulation on health insurance has a high risk of losing suitable contextual information. This is due to a lack of detailed information about its origin, how it was collected, constraints on its use, detailed specifications for data formats, and organisation of the data. To promote more complete representation of the data, and to ensure discoverability, access to and preservation of data and metadata (as complete as possible) must be ensured. Some of these metadata components may be more familiar than others.

> To support the establishment of *melesi* health insurance in Southeast Sulawesi, we interviewed relevant village heads and the potential network through a focus group discussion with communities in four villages. The collected data is primary data directly obtained from interviews and focus group discussions. The limitation that can be identified since the beginning of the programme is the lack of government support. This is because the implementation of this programme coincided with the election of the head of the Konawe Selatan district, so the people assumed that the programme was part of a political process. (LAHA)

To ensure that data is useful to local communities and policy makers, it is imperative for the richness of the codification that contextual information is collected along with the data itself. For the knowledge holders and data providers (who may be the same person), this can mean a significant amount of effort. But it is important that those most familiar with its content and context develop this information. Through the process of describing documented forms of local observations and knowledge using metadata, providers help to ensure that the data can be understood, managed and appropriately distributed, along with as much contextual information as possible. Local knowledge brings meaning to social phenomena.

The first challenge in processing local knowledge is generally associated with the nature of space and its significance, that local knowledge is largely hidden, lying tacit and dormant within communities (Campbell and Marshall, 2000). Researchers often find it difficult to be confident in selecting the right informants, actions and situations that will lead them to the essential information. The BIGS's study highlights the role of myths in forest conservation in Central Java and reported that they had to change the description of the myths as a result of inconsistencies from different informants about the what, when, where, who and why of myths in the community.

> In the field, researchers need to adapt to become part of the community. This is done to obtain information, because at first, the community will not be open. Researchers need to show that they have the same thinking and feeling as the community, in order for them to provide information. For example, when outsiders ask whether there are myths in a village, the villagers will not reveal that information. But, as our field researcher was a local organiser who not only understands, but also preserves the local culture of the research site, such 'mythical' information was shared. (BIGS)

A second challenge is around language and linguistic diversity. This is not merely a matter of communication and interpretation. Indigenous peoples and local communities possess distinctive nomenclatures and taxonomies with respect to biodiversity; these lexicons are often technically complex for talking about observations, evidence and proof (Thaman et al, 2013). Knowledge about climate in Indramayu, West Java, is embedded in indigenous and local concepts. It can be neither captured nor conveyed with any rigour by a simple translation into scientific concepts. Studies from other locations reported similar challenges.

> Another role played by civil society is translating local knowledge into a language that can be easily understood by policy makers, including promoting the creation of a dialogue space in order for the local people to regain control over that space and their natural resources. Civil society has a duty to bridge local knowledge so that policy makers can comprehend it. This is not an easy task. A number of scientific methodologies, such as mapping, participative ethnography, participative rural study, barefoot engineering, barefoot observation and recording phenomena through local languages are methods commonly used by civil society to communicate local knowledge to outsiders, especially to policy makers. (Pikul)

> In practice, efforts to adapt to the community's culture can be made by wearing the same attire, speaking/using the same language and being respectful to the community's culture. As our researchers understood the local culture, they easily adapted their research approach (in language, clothing or ways to contact informants). They used visualisation as a tool to gather knowledge from villagers. BIGS made an animated film based on their research findings. This film was shown to the people to obtain, among others, their input on its validity. Visualisation has been proven to stimulate people's excitement to provide opinions and input. (BIGS)

A third challenge relates to the fact that knowledge is also embodied in areas that are 'value-based', such as morality and spirituality. It puts outside partners in a difficult situation. For example, in the case of whale hunting in Lembata, fishers were challenged by tension between the traditions of the whale hunt for livelihood, and the emerging marine conservation movement, both of which they recognised as important.

There are two important debates in relation to the whaling tradition versus the tourist industry. First is the conflict between the interests of whale hunting and cultural conservation. Some people think it is crucial to preserve their whaling culture, because this tradition is not commercial in nature. Whale hunting is carried out for all of the people in Lembata, not only for individuals. 'We are not ignoring the environment, but culture also needs to be developed', they say. Whale hunting in Lamalera village is a tradition passed down through generations. Despite receiving criticism from environmentalists, the community sees its culture as appropriate, because the whole cultural and social dimension of the people of Lembata is enshrined in this whale hunting tradition. Eliminating this cultural practice would be the same as destroying the socio-economic tradition of the Lembata people. The idea of whale conservation among Lamalera people is a 'foreign' one, whereas cultural conservation is 'local knowledge'.

The second debate concerns the contestation between communal and non-commercial traditional values and a market-oriented tourism logic. The government's policy on tourism in Lamalera is viewed as a threat to the traditional values of the people. The relatively conflict-free tradition of distributing hunting yields is in contrast to distributing 'money' from the tourism industry. The people have learned to be commercial when it comes to the tourism industry. For example, based on indigenous discussions in 2015, visitors carrying video cameras were charged Rp 3 million (US$225), and those with cameras, Rp 150,000 (US$11). Those who look at the fish capturing activity, even a glance, will be charged Rp 150,000 (USD$11). The problem lies in the distribution system, as the traditional distribution structure is not applicable in a monetised system. (Poros Photo)

From the perspective of the position and role of local knowledge, these debates show the vulnerability of local knowledge when faced with external knowledge or economic logic. Many people have codified local knowledge about this tradition, but the challenge is in the next process, namely how people can engage in a dialogue from different perspectives (for example whale conservation) and also market instruments such as the tourism industry. In these cases, communities might need 'intermediaries' to bridge dialogue and the adaptation processes.

Conclusions

Our partners identified five common trends and shocks in which the utility and maintenance of local knowledge is challenged, following the framework introduced by Blaikie, as cited in FAO (no date):

1. Areas of very rapid population growth, with a concomitant reduction in resources caused by external pressures, may require adaptations of new technologies to increase production and diversify livelihoods. Climate change adaptation in Indramayu and *sasi* coastal fisheries in Maluku are examples of the challenges created by rapid socio-economic and environmental changes. These adaptations require a rapid learning of new skills. In this situation, local knowledge would have to develop, and adapt very quickly, to respond to the challenges.
2. The studies by POLGOV about local communities and mining in East Nusa Tenggara province and by LK3 on river-based communities in South Kalimantan highlight circumstances in which rapid migration to a particular area meant that the repertoire of knowledge for agricultural and pastoral production and environmental conservation were out of focus with a new set of environmental conditions, opportunities and constraints. The

socio-economic structures creating this knowledge faced fracturing and contradictory additions as new migrants arrived. Resettlement programmes introduced by the city government of Banjarmasin provided one example of these circumstances. People found themselves in a new situation, where their local knowledge was no longer relevant. These types of shocks can lead to the complete loss of existing local knowledge (in both old and new communities).

3. Disasters and other extreme events cause a disjuncture, both materially and culturally. This often causes shocks to the knowledge system. Such instances are both opportunistic and limiting. A relevant example is the two case studies in Aceh (YKU and PKPM) where the knowledge system's existence was threatened because many people possessing the knowledge were lost in the tsunami of 2004; at the same time, this event also provided triggers for revitalisation and the introduction of various community-based initiatives, often introduced by international development partners.

4. There are other processes of slow-moving environmental change, such as climate change, widespread deforestation or land degradation, that challenge the resilience and adaptability of local knowledge systems. The farmer climate change adaptation programme in Indramayu, the river-based community in South Kalimantan, forest conservation in Central Java, mining exploitation in Flores and water management in Kupang, East Nusa Tenggara, are examples of adaptation to environmental conditions. In those situations, an innovation and adaptation process must take place to adjust the system to challenges that arise. These are examples showing how local people manage to adapt their practices and knowledge to changing environments; often the result is greater diversity because the adaption process is highly contextual and constitutes a co-evaluative process, with the changing physical and social environment.

5. Rapid commercialisation and economic shocks may also undermine local knowledge. The cases of whale hunting in Lembata, East Nusa Tenggara and coastal fisheries in Maluku confirm the influence of rapid commercialisation and economic shocks on local

knowledge, which led to tensions between community groups, local government and businesses.

The potency of inequality within local knowledge (see page 103) has significant implications for its research methodology and its use for development work, including policy making. Access to knowledge is governed by culturally specific rules and procedures that are not immune to inequality challenges. Attention to gender equality and social inclusion in all local knowledge processes is critical to understanding the knowledge itself and how to use it for policy.

All these aspects present challenges to local knowledge systems, including the methodology to document and process local knowledge. However, impacts are not just negative. Farmers' innovation in Indramayu in agro-meteorology, and the community-based health financing system in Southeast Sulawesi are good examples of successful adaptations and innovations that have resulted from external challenges. The challenges described earlier will lead to adaptation. This in turn will increase existing diversity of forms and actors. The most important lesson from these challenges is that an adequate stock of knowledge about the broader context must be taken into account when trying to understand existing local knowledge. Understanding broader socio-cultural and environmental contexts is critical to giving the meanings of the proxies of local knowledge, or local skills, events, rituals and behaviours.

SIX

Using local knowledge in policy making

Adopted policies are often not the policies that technical evidence recommends as the best or even the second best. Policies are made not just on the basis of technical evidence, but also under the influence of non-technical forces, such as public opinion and political pressure. As discussed in Chapter Two, policies must be put into practice in a society which somehow must accommodate the vested interests of various pressure and special interest groups. The influence of these non-technical factors is important, somewhat non-transparent and non-systematic, in both developing and developed countries. The landscape of these influential technical and non-technical factors shapes constraints as well as opportunities for the use of knowledge in policy making.

How is local knowledge communicated?

As we saw in the previous chapter, partners' local knowledge is far more complex and varied than scientific knowledge. It can be both tacit and explicit, and both individual and shared, making it harder to communicate in the formal legalistic policy-making process. This feature shapes the way research partners communicate local knowledge for influencing policy-making processes.

Partners' first strategy in communicating local knowledge is a process of 'local knowledge reproduction': identifying and codifying different types and expressions of local knowledge into tangible products that are 'communication-friendly'. These are then made available to a wide variety of end users including local community members, scientists, policy makers and the general public. Each of these user groups may have different levels of access and need information in a different form.

The use of local knowledge depends on the type of knowledge product and the datasets documented. Local knowledge datasets and products vary: tables of observations, works of art (graphic, music and sculpture), photographs, local gazetteers, local dictionaries and other linguistic materials, local weather station data, maps and transcripts of recordings. Despite this variety, most of the use of local knowledge as reported by partners is in the form of text, articles and audiovisual media, as the key target audiences are the public and government/policy makers.

> In our study of water management in Timor, we noted that there is still work to be done to build understanding and dialogue across the community (among different clans) and between the community and policy makers. Outstanding issues include collective arrangements of water management, conflict resolution mechanisms and minimum recognition of management rights, tiered management, knowledge on the history of water sources, and adoption of a water resources management structure. Therein lie the challenges of engaging other institutions to perform a collaborative and collective assessment, and to change the paradigm of decision makers to understand and accept that local knowledge on community-based water management contains various values, norms and positive beliefs that preserve the sustainability of water management, both upstream and downstream. (Pikul)

The communication strategies of partners described in the reports included a wide variety of media, languages, forums and communication processes to maximise participation and learning from and by indigenous and local knowledge holders. PKPM in Aceh reported that its first public hearing for policy advocacy with a local government was regulated by the use of formal language, which included technical terms and certain patterns of communication.

> We intensively created personal and institutional approaches with policy makers and convinced them that what is being fought for is very useful for the people. What is more important and has added value in the process is the power of the emotional bond. This bond breaks down bureaucratic layers that sometimes make discussion difficult. Informal approaches in certain situations will make things easier in the policy-making process. Some of our communication efforts with relevant institutions and the district parliament (DPRK) have yielded results. DPRK is very supportive of efforts to integrate local knowledge on rice field agriculture into local policy. (PKPM Aceh)

Through this format, they found that the bureaucratic layers did not recognise everyday informal language of lay people where local knowledge is embedded. Rather, it created distorted communication in policy deliberation processes in which individuals of higher social status used expert voices to overshadow local knowledge and views. This distortion of communication resulted in an exclusion of local knowledge. Many local participants censored themselves, as they did not have the self-confidence to express their own knowledge in the face of expert opinion that sometimes disparaged local knowledge. To address this, PKPM changed the format and setting of the meeting and community facilitators played a greater role in facilitating the dialogue.

> In a less-than-supportive political structure, personal approach and individual communication are two important keys in successfully influencing policy. High quality research evidence is not enough to influence policy. There must be a dynamic at play within the political structure. Even in the local context,

this is an important lesson in influencing policy. Policy actors can support this research outcome and be important actors in our view. We conducted regular approaches to the head of Aceh Besar DPRK, the vice district head, and several directors and staff of relevant offices. Through close individual relationships, these policy actors have pushed issues forward in forums where they are involved, including in programme discussion between the executive and legislative branches. (PKPM Aceh)

With regard to policy advocacy, partners reported organising public hearings as an instrument for incorporating local knowledge into government planning processes. Although channels used to approach government are different in different regions (for example, in Aceh with the district planning agency, in Southeast Sulawesi through the Bureau of Law at the district head's office, and in Kendal, Central Java, through the DPRD), they shared the approach of framing local knowledge as 'local sentiment'. This celebrated local wisdom in a political culture of regional autonomy that often honours the local.

The other approach implemented by local partners to communicate with local knowledge-to-policy makers has been to emphasise that local knowledge not only frames the boundaries and possibilities of local policy, but also shapes the interpretations of policy legitimacy. However, there are structural and administrative constraints to pushing local knowledge in policy decisions. These constraints include the formal procedures for policy-making mechanisms, representation issues and budgeting procedures, as in the following case reported by YKU in Aceh.

> A beneficial change for people who contribute labour to economic development activities was delivered by the Beng Mawah Micro-Finance Institution. The change was initiated by civil society organisation activists in Aceh. The Beng Mawah Micro-Finance Institution provides access to capital for its members to start a venture in agriculture or farming, or a home industry. A capital loan is given without collateral, with profit

sharing of 70:30, higher than the general profit sharing of 50:50. The Beng Mawah Micro-Finance Institution has distributed around Rp 333 million (US$25,000) to 45 members. Even though it continues to grow, it still faces challenges, such as limited availability of capital, meaning people have to wait for more than one saving and loan cycle (one year) to apply for credit. In addition, the limited business scale causes the income of the institution to be limited; it cannot afford to pay staff professionally. The Aceh Province Community Empowerment Agency needs to encourage village government to prepare a village regulation to ensure that profit sharing is professional, honest, fair and in line with Islamic *shariya* law. (YKU)

Another issue documented by research partners is people's motivation to participate in public policy-making processes. Partner organisations reported that people act only when they feel that their position is under threat because of a public policy. This explains why local knowledge on sustainable water ecosystem management in Torong Besi, East Nusa Tenggara, became a driver for the people to respond to a government policy that allows mining activities in their livelihood areas. Communities in Torong Besi are less interested in participating in government-managed development planning forums (known as *musrenbang*) because they do not reflect local knowledge, and in some cases even conflict with local conditions. Under a state-led bottom-up development planning regime like *musrenbang*, where local aspirations are often invisible at a higher level, the question arises: which participatory practices are most efficacious in capturing local knowledge and incorporating it into plans? The case from BIGS in Central Java shows that local knowledge can make normative contributions to environmental and development planning, and toward enhanced procedural democracy. This is the result of the incorporation of previously excluded and marginalised voices into technical research and decision-making processes, particularly in technocratic decision-making processes where expertise tends to exclude people.

The focus is on the social and cultural history of Kendal. The form is an event on the anniversary of the district, and an art festival. Traditional values, including respect for nature, and ceremonies have not yet been celebrated; according to the Culture and Tourism Agency, this is due to the absence of a local partner that can be asked to work together and use the local government's budget to promote traditional values. Therefore, the Culture and Tourism Office requested that the BIGS team in Kendal establish an indigenous institution. The institution would be added as a partner. The following year, it would receive funding in the form of support for cultural activities. BIGS views this as a promising opportunity to promote institutional, culture-based forest preservation advocacy in Kendal district. (BIGS)

In communicating their local observations and knowledge, partners demonstrate a shared understanding that they need to go beyond the 'exoticism' of local wisdom to its utility in managing community life. Simply attempting to capture local observations and knowledge and publish them may fail to adequately represent the knowledge, and even lead to a 'commodification' of local knowledge, as in the following experiences from PUSKA UI:

Translating scientific arguments, findings and evidence into a policy brief to develop learning among policy makers is not easy. Without strong support of the agro-meteorologist on the scientific arguments and findings about climate change and its implications for agriculture, and the realities shown by farmers themselves, it would not have been possible to convince policy makers of the importance of introducing science field shops. Climate change is not a negotiable subject. It is a reality, yet it is beyond lay people's understanding without knowledge transfer and climate services provided by scientists and responsible authorities (for example, the National Agency for Meteorology, Climatology and Geo-physics). For policy makers, being flexible in adjusting policies under emerging, unexpected or unusual circumstances has not been part of the 'habitus'. The question is the extent to which 'responsive and flexible governance' has been part of the bureaucratic culture to respond to emerging phenomena such as climate change, which is already having an impact on the environment and on people's livelihoods. We realised, therefore, that translating the complex phenomena into language understood by policy makers was a matter of urgency. Again, the work of the agro-meteorological expert was crucial and an inter-disciplinary collaboration was necessary. Translating the scientific explanations into understandable Bahasa Indonesia presented narratively was also very demanding work that needed hours of experience and learning.

The challenge faced by a researcher in local knowledge is how to effectively communicate study findings to policy makers. The science field shops not only provide practical solutions to farmers, they also mediate between relevant parties from different levels of the system. For example, science field shops need to convince the government and policy makers that providing climate services and other services to farmers in an appropriate and timely manner enables them to adapt to climate change. PUSKA UI, along with the Rainfall Observation Club, holds workshops and communicates science field shops to the local government. This communication can be in the form of community radio, social media, video or policy briefs. These activities strengthen networks and engage policy makers. Farmers can anticipate and make some changes, but for policy making and policy influence, they cannot do it alone, they need help to engage with and influence government.

We [PUSKA UI] initiated the up-scaling movement and dissemination of science field shops and agro-meteorological learning through community radio broadcasting in Nunuk village, Indramayu. We continued this by also initiating a new broadcast in the northwest of Indramayu. In East Lombok, the farmers already had their tradition of social gatherings in an open hut called a *Berugaq*. Farmer-to-farmer knowledge transfer had been happening since the formation of the Indramayu Rainfall Observation Club through rural communication networks. Besides the rural knowledge transfer and communication technologies developed in the past six months, we also initiated social media and video productions. Farmers also used Facebook and Instagram, which allowed other farmers and the general public to access their seasonal scenarios, news and activities around agro-meteorological learning. PUSKA will make a monthly editorial plan, which can be accessed by both the PUSKA and Sirius Labs (an information technology and social media organisation). Later, Sirius Labs will upload photos, articles and seasonal scenarios in line with the editorial plan on Facebook and Instagram. (PUSKA UI)

Framing local knowledge as 'good practice' without context presents the risk of removing important social and cultural information about the origins of the knowledge, how the data were created, and appropriate and acceptable uses of the data. A good example is Poros Photo's study of the whaling traditions in Lembata, East Nusa Tenggara. They attempted to communicate the message that this tradition was integral to the community's way of life and indeed its world view; abolishing it would end not only their livelihood, but the very thing upon which their sense of community and identity is built. Poros Photo followed the daily lives of the villagers of Lamalera and took pictures related to the whaling activities. A photo and film exhibition was organised and a photo essay book was published to communicate the message that the indigenous practice of community whaling is different from commercial whaling. Responses to the Poros Photo exhibition and publication varied. Some of the responses indicated that the communication strategy was effective. By going beyond the simple documentation of local observations and knowledge, the use of interactive exhibitions and multimedia presented new possibilities for recording and sharing local observations and knowledge. The audio and video recordings documented observations, knowledge and narratives as told by knowledge holders and communities in the language of their choice. To add a visual dimension, Poros Photo provided photographs and other visualisations to further complement the knowledge documentation process. Amplifying the message and the movement, working through media (including social media) is another effective communication strategy.

Who to influence

In general, in their efforts to influence policy making, partners do not directly engage key policy makers. Instead, they work through agents – people surrounding key policy makers, such as influential legislators and administrators, as well as community decision makers or influential local leaders and influential citizens. The agents of change with whom the partners engage vary in terms of positions and roles within knowledge-to-policy processes. In areas where traditional structures and institutions exist and remain influential, the key agents of change to influence are indigenous people's leaders and councils. These groups function as intermediary organisations to reach policy makers. If policy makers believe the public needs to be educated in the ways and knowledge of professional experts to meaningfully participate in development decisions, partners first influence local university scientists to have an alliance to strengthen their 'scientific' legitimacy. What they offer to the university scientists is social legitimacy and access to data in the community.

> Even though the mechanisms we used supported our efforts to influence policy makers, this did not necessarily mean that policy makers would accept our arguments and evidence. Farmers had traditionally been considered 'objects and targets' of all government programmes, rather than government counterparts in achieving national or local objectives in agricultural development. Therefore, acceptance of farmers' stories and evidence was not to be expected immediately. In responding to scientists' and farmers' arguments, policy makers would refer to their own perceptions, ideas and programmes which, in their

eyes, proved to be 'right' and 'effective' in producing changes in farming practices. Critiques and comments, instead of listening and trying to understand the scientists' and farmers' arguments, were common. Although on one hand they accepted the importance of the climate change issue, on the other hand they had a responsibility to achieve the main objective – increasing productivity. Addressing the 'danger' and 'imminent threat' of the consequences of climate change against the main objective of achieving high productivity, supported by evidence, had to be considered by both scientists and farmers in their presentations and voices. The visual media, such as the film screening, photo exhibitions and farmers' own products, together with the scientists' PowerPoint presentations, were appropriate ways to influence policy makers. However, without the involvement of farmers themselves, any efforts to influence policy makers would not yield sufficient results. (PUSKA UI)

Locality and place are relevant to local knowledge organisations, especially in their efforts to institutionalise specific local knowledge in public policy. This is because 'the local' is seen as simply a backdrop for action. For example, *melesi*, the community mechanism for sharing the burden in Southeast Sulawesi, was originally applied in Ranomeeto sub-district and is being scaled up at Konawe Selatan through a district regulation. Another case involves the Bappeda office in Aceh Besar, which is developing operational guidelines to implement the *mawah* system in the district.

> Various stakeholders and important actors with information are engaged at multiple stages. They include village leaders, religious leaders (*Imuem Mukim, keuchik, keujruen*, MAA, P3A) and agriculture educators. The objective is to obtain information comprehensively, according to the facts on the ground. *Imuem Mukim* (a sub-district level leader) and *keuchik* (the head of a village/*gampong*) are important figures in exploring local knowledge. They also act as intermediaries who can

communicate local knowledge to the government. The Aceh Province Planning Agency, Aceh Indigenous Council and relevant offices discuss the mechanisms to implement *mawah* in the poverty eradication policy, the distribution of village funds and village cash transfers from provincial government, as well as the *gampong* economic empowerment programme from relevant institutions. The Aceh government recognises and supports the existence of *mawah* by drafting a *Qanun* (Local Regulation), so that *mawah*, as a heritage of Aceh, does not become marginalised in its place of origin. (YKU)

When the policy-making process and local political context were closed, partner organisations tried to influence the public through 'popular education' to create public pressure on policy makers, as in the case below.

In a monolithic political structure, with relatively homogenous political actors and very dominant elites, the policy-making process is determined by a handful of people. In this situation, we conducted popular education to create significantly stronger public pressure and consolidation of various parties with the same concerns around collective action. Consolidation of collective actions is useful as an education process. The experiences from Belu and Manggarai demonstrated that a number of actors and intermediaries played serious roles in promoting the engagement of local people and transforming local knowledge into policies on the extractive industry. These intermediaries do more than just transform local knowledge from tacit to explicit knowledge; they strive to consolidate collective action to improve natural resource management in their respective areas. (POLGOV)

As we saw in Chapters Two and Five, religion can be a key element in shaping local knowledge, serving to preserve a group's unity, as well as being a medium through which identity conflicts are reflected and negotiated. The extent to which religious leaders are engaged in policy-making processes varies greatly from one location to another. For example, the report by POLGOV shows how the Archbishop of Ruteng (and the Catholic Church's international network) is one of the more influential groups in the policy-making process in Manggarai and East Nusa Tenggara. Therefore, in the policy advocacy work for anti-mining, POLGOV and other civil society organisations engaged religious leaders to influence the policy-making process in Manggarai. Aceh is another good example of how partners could build the support of religious and *adat* groups.

> The Aceh Traditional Adat Council or *Majelis Adat* Aceh (MAA) is one of the stakeholders within the organisational structure of the Aceh government. MAA is actively promoting Islam and local knowledge in government policies. The example is from the provincial level, where MAA has promoted local knowledge through the issuance of Governor Regulation (*Pergub*) 45/2015 on the Role of *Keujruen Blang* in irrigation management. In this regulation, the term P3A is omitted and is replaced by *Keujruen Blang*, showing that this Governor Regulation has very much acknowledged local knowledge. Furthermore, MAA included the empowerment of the *Keujruen Blang* traditional institution as one of its programmatic focuses for 2016. (PKPM Aceh)

The politics of local knowledge to policy

Our partners showed different mechanisms for using local knowledge and understanding the local political context to influence policy-making processes in different political-economy settings. In general, they implemented the following strategies and approaches:

Relationship-based influence

Partners and communities sometimes mobilised personal networks to approach policy makers and people surrounding them, building trust and then following the procedural/legal process to formalise policy changes. With this approach, the credibility and authoritative power of their arguments were based on the intermediary's personal power, as in the following cases.

> We intensively create personal and institutional approaches with policy makers and convince them that what we are fighting for is very useful for the people. What is more important and has added value to the process is the power of the emotional bond. This can break bureaucratic layers that sometimes make discussion difficult. Informal approaches in certain situations will make things easier in the policy-making process. Some of our communication efforts with relevant institutions and DPRK have yielded results. They are very supportive of efforts to integrate local knowledge on rice field agriculture into local policy. (PKPM Aceh)

> Personal, face-to-face communication with intended policy makers proved useful and effective in building up a mutual understanding and in finding common ground to develop a policy and programmes supporting science field shops. We experienced this through our personal communication with the vice-head of East Lombok, and the head of the Agricultural Extension Office in Indramayu. (PUSKA UI)

> Through interviews, we build communication and approaches – this is not done during working hours. Sometimes we communicate in the interviewee's home, making the process more fluid and relaxed. The intensity of communication is established through personal approaches to selected policy-making stakeholders within the local government and DPRD, outside of formal activities, for example, by visiting their office. This was implemented to promote the recommended proposal being developed, and to learn the response and views of the stakeholders. Local civil society partners and networks can play a crucial part in helping build trust with stakeholders, both in

local government and with indigenous leaders. We conveyed policy briefs in a multi-stakeholder discussion. Responses were positive from the participating stakeholders, such as local secretariat staff, Bappeda, the Environmental Agency, the Marine Affairs and Fisheries Office, members of DPRD, indigenous *adat* and religious leaders. The meeting agreed on recommendations from the study, and requested the team follow up these recommendations by converting them into an academic paper to gain a comprehensive and deep understanding of the concept, objective and goals. (PATTIRO)

Local knowledge as an 'electoral asset'

In a decentralised polity such as Indonesia with competitive local elections, local knowledge can be used to convince decision makers of community practices. Advocates rely on the political dimension of local knowledge as a manifestation of an interest group's aspiration, instead of the technical ('efficiency') explanatory factor. When Pikul brought evidence that local water systems were more effective to sub-national authorities in East Nusa Tenggara, it was not how strong the technical solution was that won the day, but more because the system was accepted by a large number of people who represented a significant electoral asset. This message made local politicians become more conscious of local solutions.

In many cases, local practices were communicated as an aspiration or shared concern of policy makers' voters. This 'politicisation' of local knowledge is possible because local knowledge may serve to constitute social identities, which is one of the main bases of political support.

> In the knowledge-to-policy process, the capacity to identify, produce and disseminate knowledge produced by, from and through the community is necessary, but not sufficient. Experience often demonstrates that the capacity to establish political strategy and tactics is a determining factor. On one hand, such political capacity is the ability to identify and explore

opportunities in political structures, engage in political education at the grassroots level and establish awareness and public pressure through collective action. On the other hand, it is the ability to negotiate with parties relevant and influential to the policy process. This political capacity is as important as the technocratic capacity to produce knowledge that will be used as evidence in the policy process through a series of scientific methods that are deemed valid and logical. (POLGOV)

The understanding of policy makers and other stakeholders on the importance of local knowledge in formulating policies has improved. An example of this is the involvement of the Aceh Besar Vice District Head who cooperated with various parties to revitalise Keujruen Blang. This included opening political access and lines to make it easier for PKPM to conduct advocacy on the research result. Based on the interview with PKPM researchers, the Vice District Head was willing to offer support, as this would give him an opportunity to raise his popularity for the next election. The district parliament (DPRK) of Aceh Besar included PKPM's policy notes in the local 2017 legislation programme and the chair of the local parliament ordered relevant commissions to cooperate with PKPM in drafting a district regulation (Qanun) on the Empowerment of Keujruen Blang. (PKPM Aceh)

Local wisdom is an important element when making policies to establish an environmentally friendly city to adapt to global climate change. The Banjarmasin House of Representatives agreed to listen to LK3 on several occasions, on issues such as river management, *lanting* houses, building permits and the establishment, arrangement and use of river boundaries, including those of former rivers. These local regulations, as recommended by LK3 research, need to be revised according to the cultural characteristics of the Banjar people.

There are, however, risks with this approach. In the political sphere, it is a fine line between localism, populism and prejudice. Even though we did not find any outright instance of this in our ten localities, it is a common phenomenon in Indonesia. A study by an Indonesian human rights group (ELSAM, 2008) presents the implementation of local regulations in three districts (Garut, Bulukumba and Padang). The study finds that many regulations, although they used community aspirations and local wisdom as key references, were often exclusive and discriminatory. For example, Local Regulation No 6/2003 of Bulukumba, forces the Toraja indigenous group to register as Muslims to claim land or to marry. What we did find in our studies, though, were instances in which local knowledge was monopolised by certain community groups to the exclusion of others, reinforcing inequalities. A pattern of gathering, codifying, analysing and translating local knowledge into public policy may draw local knowledge into an institutionalisation trap, moving away from the locality concept of local knowledge, into populism and discrimination against outsiders. We need to be careful not to romanticise local knowledge, or take it at face value.

Improving community participation in policy implementation decisions

Communities and partners can put pressure on planners to find new ways of fusing the expertise of scientists with insights from the local knowledge of communities. Partners worked with the communities facing the most serious environmental risks to challenge the distinctions of experts and lay people.

> Fundamentally, a policy should be relevant to the needs and preferences of the public. Therefore, evidence is needed. Traditionally, most evidence has come from organisations or institutions whose expertise in identifying and producing knowledge in a logical and scientific manner is recognised, such as civil society organisations, think tanks and others. We cannot ignore the fact that evidence may come from people's experience through their various backgrounds, both those formally trained and those who have learned from daily experience. (POLGOV)

> LAHA facilitator's conducted 'Community Aspiration Networks' (*Jaring Aspirasi Masyarakat*) through multiple approaches (organising group discussions, interviewing hospital inpatients and conducting household surveys) to obtain evidence and experience on a government health insurance (BPJS) funding policy. LAHA collected the real costs paid by BPJS participants, then submitted this as evidence to be negotiated with BPJS officers, the health office and the local government to find a contextual financing solution. This activity encouraged the local government to bridge the gap between the calculation of BPJS health fees and the real needs of the people by providing a complementary service to local health insurance. (LAHA)

There were also cases where the dominant view of community knowledge complemented the work of experts. The task of partners was to convince policy makers by integrating local knowledge with university-generated scientific knowledge and in the process, as discussed in Chapter Two (page 40–41), improve the quality of public policy and chances of implementation. Partners facilitate a 'hybridising' of professional discourse with local experience, and ultimately promote the 'scientification' of local knowledge on the one hand, and wider democratic legitimacy for scientific decisions on the other. This strategy was chosen because promoting the message that local knowledge is good is not always easy. Partners reported some critical responses asking, 'If indigenous knowledge is so good, why is the community owning the knowledge so poor?'

> Since undertaking the research, PUSKA UI researchers have worked with communities. They have used available scientific and local knowledge to implement appropriate climate change adaptation actions. This has led to enhanced knowledge and awareness through the production of community-based climate change adaptation materials integrating scientific and local expertise, including field demonstrations, videos and posters. Community members and government officials met at a science

field shop to discuss the research results and their application in policy and practice. This was especially important in light of unpredicted temperatures and rainfall fluctuations that are causing concern for farmers. It also created opportunities to link bottom-up knowledge with top-down support. We learned that advocacy work in promoting science field shops as part of government policies needs to be supported strongly by scientific evidence. Evidence has been based on recent local empirical phenomena familiar to farmers and policy makers, and not merely on comparative knowledge and discoveries from elsewhere in the world. Farmers' own discoveries constituted a significant part of strengthening scientists' arguments and ideas. (PUSKA UI)

As part of an advocacy strategy on environmental and mining activities in Belu, East Nusa Tenggara, POLGOV supported the affected communities to work with several national NGO networks: indigenous rights (AMAN), environment (WALHI) and anti-mining (JATAM) groups. They found several mechanisms effective in influencing policy, such as using existing local networks – networks of local scientists, local NGOs and local agricultural extension staff. The farmers themselves often played an important role.

The choice of organising a communication forum in the form of a 'workshop' instead of a 'seminar' was beneficial in bringing evidence-based knowledge to the forum and in providing opportunities for dialogue among all parties. The involvement of knowledge producers themselves from both scientific and farming communities in representing their experience, knowledge and evidence, and in voicing their arguments in the dialogue with policy makers, proved beneficial in influencing the latter's thinking, knowledge and perspectives. An arena for presenting evidence and discussing arguments is not common in the tradition of 'top-down' technology transfer when bureaucrats aim to transfer techniques rather than knowledge. (POLGOV)

Another mechanism partners used to influence policy-making processes was to provide a 'reality check' or feedback to policy makers about the impacts of existing policies. One of the approaches under this mechanism was to provide empirical evidence about 'distributive justice'. Partners highlighted the problems, alternatives, opportunities and solutions. For example, by revealing who gets what and how much from the tourism industry in Lembata, communities could highlight the disproportionate burdens and benefits they experienced from tourism every day. When community members asked whether the Lembata district policy on tourism fairly distributed the benefits and burdens, they were asking who the winners and the losers were, thus providing a reality check on the local impact of the policy. The Lembata government issued a district regulation on tourism management to protect local revenue sharing mechanisms. In the *melesi* case in Southeast Sulawesi, partners collected data and experiences from community members on the use of the government health insurance scheme (BPJS). They then organised a seminar with stakeholders to present the community's perspective on the implementation of BPJS. The seminar provided empirical evidence about the limitations and challenges of the BPJS policy and how the *melesi* local system could complement the formal system.

SEVEN

Conclusion: improving public policy through local assets

The use of knowledge and evidence in public policy has been a popular topic of discussion over the past decade. Much research and many projects have focused on how evidence can be better used in public policy to improve the potential for policy success. Policy makers do not rely solely on evidence to make decisions. They must take political considerations into account as well as pressures from communities, the business sector and the opposition. But when they do rely on evidence, they tend to privilege scientific evidence. As a result, holders of local knowledge have to be strategic in getting their messages into the policy process.

The evidence-informed policy literature has focused largely on formal scientific evidence – how can it be used, how can science get better at communicating its evidence in ways policy makers can use, how can policy makers be better informed about seeking evidence and interpreting it? While some have acknowledged that other forms of evidence should also be considered, little attention has focused on how to achieve this or what we mean by other forms of evidence. An important exception to this is the work supported by the Centers for Disease Control (Puddy and Wilkins, 2011), which defines three types of evidence: the best and most rigorous research evidence (what we term scientific knowledge); the most knowledgeable experience and expertise (professional knowledge); and values and perspectives of the person or community affected by the intervention (local knowledge). Here, they do not go far enough in our view, as they treat local knowledge as values and perspectives rather than as an actual source of knowledge.

This volume, based on the experience generated through ten diverse case studies of the influence of local knowledge on public policy, is a contribution to opening up discussion of what we mean by other forms of knowledge and how their influence is generated.

We started from the premise that local knowledge is an important consideration in public policy and that we wanted to understand more about how it was important and what we could learn from that about the potential of local knowledge to grow its influence. We situated local knowledge as one of three types of knowledge: scientific, professional and local. Each uses a different evidence base and each plays a role. Scientific evidence comes from research and pilot programmes that demonstrate the value of a particular intervention. Professional knowledge comes from a mix of the evidence from science, the experience of the professionals, and their knowledge of formal and informal systems – in other words bringing the evidence and the context together. Local knowledge comes from the history and experience of citizens and communities in how to survive and grow in their own settings. We wanted to understand more about why that mattered and what implications it holds for the future of improving the contribution of knowledge to better public policies.

The debate around how knowledge influences public policy increasingly recognises that it is not only about 'what works' so that we know which policies we can apply, but also about what works for whom and in what context (Pawson, 2006; Carden, 2009; Cartwright and Hardie, 2012). This is a recognition that context and power matter a great deal in public policy. Different places and different communities, even different groups within communities – men and women, young and old, rich and poor – are differentially affected by a new policy.

CONCLUSION: IMPROVING PUBLIC POLICY THROUGH LOCAL ASSETS

What we have seen through these case studies is that local knowledge can make a powerful contribution to a better understanding of context and the differential effects of policies on different communities and in different locations, particularly where there is a strong interest in and support for the co-production of knowledge.

This recognition of differential impacts is increasingly important in Indonesia as the country moves to a much more decentralised system of governance with increasing power at the local level. There is stronger demand for policies that take into account local conditions, and less tolerance for one-size-fits-all national policies, especially in a country as diverse as Indonesia, with more than 300 cultural groups across an archipelago of over 17,000 islands. The opportunities and the needs to integrate local knowledge to adapt local policies are keenly important in this context.

Local knowledge is not, by definition, good or bad. Politics and power are at play. We saw cases where local knowledge put one clan in a position of power over other clans, as well as situations where the interpretation of local knowledge reinforces the power of one part of the community (usually men) over another, thereby reinforcing inequities. Local knowledge does not always travel well; what works in one community may not work in another, so the indiscriminate application of local knowledge to policy can have serious negative consequences, as discussed in the case of discriminatory local regulations that were said to have been inspired by local values in Chapter Six.

Like all forms of knowledge, local knowledge evolves and is affected by the world around it. It is not a return to a romantic past, but very much a modern, living, evolving knowledge that guides the evolution of communities. Even in cases where the knowledge can be traced back to the 1600s, change is ever present. It is affected by sudden events and disasters, such as the tsunami in Aceh in 2004 that wiped out communities and with them the local knowledge that guided many of the economic and social patterns of surrounding communities. It is affected by climate change that challenges traditional growing patterns. Migration, the arrival of other cultural groups, can have an impact: do norms and rules encoded in local knowledge in a particular location apply to immigrants from another region? How will they learn and adapt these rules to their ways of life? How is a clash of values managed when a whaling community becomes a tourist destination?

Not all interactions between scientific, professional and local knowledge end well, but we saw that they have the potential to contribute to much stronger policies. These are cases we can learn from to highlight some ways in which local, professional and scientific knowledge can work together to create better policies for social and economic development. The co-production of knowledge and the integration of different types of knowledge is a powerful tool in bringing evidence to policy processes. Because it gives more political legitimacy, as it is generated through community participation, co-production of knowledge will improve the policy by helping to address the feasibility of the policy in terms of what is technically feasible, politically appropriate, economically feasible and contextual.

Knowledge assets and strategies

Based on an exploration of how local knowledge is communicated and who needs to be influenced, Chapter Five illustrated three strategies used to bring local knowledge into the policy process:

1. relationship-based strategies around communicating not only with policy makers but other groups and individuals who influence them;
2. treating local knowledge as an electoral asset, presenting it as an aspiration for addressing voter concerns;
3. improving community participation through the co-production of knowledge, so that there are multiple pressures on decision makers to consider what local knowledge has to offer.

None of these strategies guarantees influence but they demonstrate the political nature of policy influence and how local knowledge holders are engaging. Some are intimidated by professional knowledge, but these cases illustrate that where local knowledge holders have the

CONCLUSION: IMPROVING PUBLIC POLICY THROUGH LOCAL ASSETS

confidence and support to engage with scientists, bureaucrats and politicians, they can make a difference. The strategies cut across the cases and demonstrate that where there is respect for (and by) local knowledge, it contributes not only to more relevant policies, but, what is important, to their implementation. At its core, local knowledge has often not been treated as an asset but as a liability that holds communities back. Successful implementation of local policies often happened when local leaders treated local forms of knowledge as important assets that needed to be politically supported.

What our cases illustrate is an important interplay between local, professional and scientific sources of knowledge. But it does not always go smoothly. Expectations, values and beliefs behind each form of knowledge influence how they interact. Here we suggest that it helps to understand this by looking at the tensions between these forms of knowledge.

Our case studies of local knowledge show that public policy making is a political-economy arena and therefore needs collaboration between technical evidence (complementary arguments between local knowledge and professional and scientific knowledge) and political efforts (participation and citizen engagement in local development processes). This complementarity has led to positive results in influencing the public policy-making process. Our case studies show that in various forms and intensities, our partners convinced local authorities to institutionalise local practices and knowledge to ensure the sustainability of the initiative. But we also found that adopted local knowledge for one practice did not necessarily make a difference to the policy-making process on other issues. Local organisations need to convince the politically appointed leader, not only the bureaucrats, that their initiative will provide value for them.

As we look at these cases, we see that there are a number of tensions at play between local knowledge and other forms of knowledge. Tensions are a way to describe the fact that 'the pursuit of multiple and competing values, ends and benefits inevitably gives rise to challenges about how to achieve balance' (Patrizi and Patton, 2009: 5). The point is not to resolve the tensions. There are no winners and losers and these tensions are not resolvable. Rather they are part of the tapestry of building knowledge. The goal is to appreciate the differences and recognise that, in bringing forms of knowledge together, the tensions need to be addressed and accommodations made. This is reflected in the respect that each has for the other and underpins strong relationships across knowledge types. The tensions described below do not operate in isolation from each other and can only be separated here for purposes of description. They interact with and affect each other. How one understands diverging interests affects all the other tensions. Five broad tensions are evident in our cases. A tension is successfully addressed where respect for the different points of view results in a co-production of knowledge that integrates the local with the scientific and professional.

Audience priority

The first tension is between scientific rigour and community participation, and between scientific rigour and the needs of the policy maker. Each audience has its own priorities and these do not always easily align. These tensions are complemented by tensions between interest in the influence of any form of knowledge on policy and the other influences at play in policy making. An aspect of audience priority is the tension between the focus on scientific disciplines and the more system-wide focus of local knowledge, and the somewhat middle ground of the policy maker who must adjudicate between the knowledge being used and the political imperatives of the day.

Problem definition

The second tension is between local problem definition in the case of local knowledge holders and the regional/national/global problem definition of policy makers and, frequently, scientists. Local knowledge is highly context driven and specific, whereas science seeks to generalise. In terms of perspective on problem definition, the scientific perspective on objectivity and dispassionate study contrasts sharply with the values-based approach that underpins local knowledge; in this respect, the policy maker tends to be pragmatic. In all forms of knowledge, we see top-down and bottom-up approaches to problem definition. This is a horizontal issue where we cannot see a clear distinction between types of knowledge, but it remains a tension in the use of knowledge.

Unit of analysis

The third broad tension relates to the unit of analysis. With local knowledge, the analysis is at the level of the community and the effects on the health and wellbeing of the community. More often, science looks at disciplinary analysis. There is tension between forms of knowledge and political feasibility, as well as between the interests and perspectives of the policy elite versus pluralism. In decisions based on the unit of analysis, when the bureaucracy attempts to create regulations based on local knowledge, it risks over-extending the reach of that local knowledge and imposing it on communities that do not adhere or agree. Matching the levels of operation is important here.

Unit of impact

Fourth, local knowledge users focus on impacts in their local communities, whereas science is interested in general knowledge, and professional knowledge users are often more interested in national or global systems. The outcomes being sought are also in tension, between outcomes in the community itself and outcomes in the growth of knowledge. For some, it is the growth of the pool of knowledge that is the most important outcome. For most local knowledge holders, the primary outcome is around improved wellbeing of their community.

Sources of knowledge

We have seen that there are two broad types of what we call local knowledge. The first is 'local wisdom' inherited through generations.

Examples of this are the *melesi* social insurance practice in Southeast Sulawesi, the *sasi* marine management practice in Maluku, and the *mawah* profit-sharing practices in Aceh. The second source is contemporary citizen knowledge. It is part of a contextual and living discourse, contested through everyday interactions and through interpretation by citizens of the multiple forms of knowledge that are part of their lived experience – the social capital that allows individuals to become citizens and establish communities. Examples of this are the new forms of agro-meteorology to adapt to climate change, the everyday forms of resistance against mining, and community-based water management in Kupang and Banjarmasin. Both of these are valid forms of local knowledge, but it is useful to differentiate between them.

New roles, new rules

Policy making should not depend solely on the judgement of professionals or be part of highly scripted consultations with largely pre-determined outcomes. Citizens should be able to question, challenge and deliberate with the government. Professionals need to become advisers, advocates, solution assemblers and brokers, not the holders of knowledge. In Chapter Three we made the argument for a 'de-professionalisation' of politics and public administration, breaking the tyranny of technique (Fischer, 2009). With a more positive spin, this is the democratisation of public policy – involving communities in public policies, decision making and the knowledge-to-policy process.

This necessitates among other things a more strategic role for local knowledge in development processes by setting conducive political and ethical conditions for development processes. This ensures that community members are adequately informed about projects under consideration; the information made available is both adequate, relevant and properly packaged; people are able to make sense of the information and it can be used as a tool in decision making. The role challenges peoples' existing representation systems so that the project is inclusive – in short, it ensures that the beliefs and lived experiences of a community can be the starting point for research about local and indigenous cultures; to use Tuhiwai Smith's (1999) book title, *Decolonizing Methodologies*.

In such a de-professionalisation paradigm, what is the new role for the experts, consultants and development projects? It is not only to provide ready-made solutions or 'best practices', or even to create more expert knowledge, however important that latter may be in this 'post-truth era'. What is more important is to assist citizens to engage in meaningful deliberations, to recognise their knowledge and give them voice. Experts and consultants also need to work further upstream, in what is sometimes referred to as the 'enabling environment', promoting a level playing field and opportunities for deliberative democracy and the co-production of knowledge. Experts and consultants can help citizens to understand and discuss the complex issues that affect their lives, using different sources of knowledge. This book has argued that local knowledge must be seen as part of political aspiration, as shared interest, rather than a separate or scientific body of knowledge. The issue is thus not one of the 'scientific codification' of knowledge, but rather about 'whose knowledge' and for what use.

Effective and more democratic state management and partnerships require improved governance practices at the local, national and international levels. Without evidence, policy makers fall back on intuition, ideology, conventional wisdom or theory (Banks, 2009: 4). As the empirical realities of globalisation, decentralisation, privatisation and democratisation have taken shape, revealing a range of outcomes, reform sequencing and process interaction has become more important. Policy reforms have become a 'dynamic combination of purposes, rules, actions, resources, incentives and behaviours leading to outcomes that can only imperfectly be predicted or controlled' (Brinkerhoff and Crosby, 2001: 5).

Going forward: a level playing field

The best policy options can be derailed if they fail to take into account other knowledge and other politics and how these might affect the policy options. We have presented several cases of this. For example, in Torong Besi in East Nusa Tenggara, the community's health and livelihood were being affected by a mining operation that impinged on local forests and polluted the river. Their attempts to bring this to the attention of authorities was failing until they began to work with an advocacy organisation that understood how to use local knowledge and combine it with scientific evidence and political pressures, ultimately leading to a change in policy. This case reminds us that it is important to link different types of knowledge as well as track the political context. In the face of persistent under-supply of water in Kupang, Pikul used local knowledge to identify sustainable approaches to water management and to integrate these with the scientific and engineering solutions needed to begin improving water supply. A third example is from PUSKA UI who worked with farmers through field schools to combine 'hard' science (agro-meteorology) with traditional knowledge of harvest patterns to address challenges around climate change. Where government-run outreach schools failed, these farmer-run science field shops, a collaboration between the University of Indonesia and local farmer associations, were more successful in working with farming communities to adapt to policy changes. Similar policy impact can also be read in our other cases.

As local knowledge does not travel well due to its time- and place-bound nature, more success is found in local policy processes than national ones. As we have discussed, various forms of local knowledge have been incorporated into local development practices, whether related to *melesi*, *mawah*, *Keujreun Blang* or customary whaling. These achievements were made possible through the support of local institutions, be they *adat* customary groups, local parliaments or community organisations. We were not able to document any cases in which these local practices were spread or replicated more broadly, beyond the local level. Maybe this is a characteristic of local knowledge – it is bound by place and time. The challenge for development partners (both national and international) is thus not one of replication of 'best practices', but rather to support communities and local governments to identify, codify and use development solutions that address shared concerns: health insurance, environmental protection, resource management and access to finance.

All types of knowledge can be seen as assets and the work of our partners overwhelmingly support that view. That is, knowledge adds value to what decisions we make, how we implement those decisions, and how we learn and improve. For all types of knowledge to be treated as assets, the tensions among them need to be identified and addressed. Where we have seen successes in these cases, accommodations were made and respect retained even where there were fundamental disagreements.

When local knowledge is treated as an asset, we see benefits both to the local knowledge itself and to society as a whole through its contributions to the policy process. This reflects a sense of mutual benefit, of the co-production of knowledge integrating local with professional and scientific knowledge. When university researchers integrated local knowledge into their work, rather than simply treating the community as a convenient place to carry out their own research, we saw benefits emerge, for example in the science field shops. When bureaucrats did the same they were able to integrate aspects of local knowledge rather than install a new and untested policy in a community, as seen in the case of water management on the island of Timor, East Nusa Tenggara.

The basic premise that we set out to prove holds: local knowledge enriches public policies. The knowledge assets that our cases brought to policy making and development options include:

- *They produce better policies*: a good example of this is the *melesi* social insurance scheme in Southeast Sulawesi.
- *They make public policies easier to accept and improve chances of implementation*: the *Keujruen Blang* customary irrigation system in Aceh served as a communal mechanism for water distribution, as well as a venue for broader conflict resolution among community members.
- *Using local knowledge opens up policy making for a new set of actors*: it democratises and de-professionalises policy making. Examples of

this are the consultations around forest management in Central Java and the social impact that local communities had on the mining industry.
- *Inclusion of under-represented and marginalised groups*: PKPM could revitalise customary farmers' associations by mobilising women in public consultations and LK3 could promote more inclusive river use by reaching out to women's groups.

How can local knowledge enrich other forms of knowledge? We have seen throughout this book that the knowledge-to-policy cycle is not actually a cycle at all: it is a much messier and more complex process, a political process taking place in Banks' 'maelstrom of political energy, vested interests and lobbying' (Banks, 2009: 9). The findings here are based on a small sample of cases and merit further verification against other cases of the use of local knowledge in public policy. Our cases suggest, however, that when we treat scientific, professional and local knowledge as all having something to offer public policy, especially policy at the local and regional level, the policy process benefits enormously. More than just knowledge contributing to policy formulation, local knowledge has played a central role in successful implementation of policies, in part because they are more grounded in the context, in part because the communities recognise the origin and purpose of the policy.

Building relationships to bridge local with scientific knowledge played a key role. We saw high value attached to scientific knowledge, but the cases also illustrate that scientific knowledge often failed in implementation. Building new water reservoirs without taking into account how the community itself managed its water supply resulted in waste and lost water resources. Bridging new technologies with traditional knowledge and approaches resulted in a much better solution. The tension between tourism and whaling needs dialogue and relationship building. Both are needed for the development of the community. Bringing them into harmony has met with some initial success but will need on-going relationship building and communication among the competing interests.

CONCLUSION: IMPROVING PUBLIC POLICY THROUGH LOCAL ASSETS

Together, these knowledge assets have improved our contextual understanding of local development processes, and have begun to restore the organic link between practical discourse and public policy by providing a forum for non-academic, but rich sources of socially relevant knowledge.

References

Ackerman, J. (2004) 'Co-governance for accountability: Beyond "exit" and "voice"', *World Development*, 32(3): 447–463.

Agrawal, A. (1995) 'Dismantling the divide between indigenous and scientific knowledge', *Development and Change*, 26(3): 413–439.

AIPI (Akademi Ilmu Pengetahuan Indonesia) (2017) 'SAINS45, Indonesian science agenda towards a century of independence', Jakarta: AIPI, www.aipi.or.id/index.php?pg=detilpublikasi&pid=58&type=2.

Andrews, M., Pritchett, L. and Woolcock, M. (2012) 'Escaping capability traps through problem-driven iterative adaptation', *Working Paper* 299, Washington, DC: Centre for Global Development, www.cgdev.org/publication/escaping-capability-traps-through-problem-driven-iterative-adaptation-pdia-working-paper.

Andrews, M., Pritchett, L. and Woolcock, M. (2017) *Building state capability: Evidence, analysis, action*, Oxford: Oxford University Press.

Antlov, H. and Hidayat, S. (2004) 'Decentralization by default in Indonesia', in P. Oxhorn, J. Tulchin and A. Selee (eds) *Decentralization, civil society, and democratic governance: Comparative perspectives from Latin America, Africa, and Asia*, Washington, DC: Woodrow Wilson Center.

Antlov, H. and Wetterberg, A. (2013) 'Citizen engagement, deliberative spaces and the consolidation of post-authoritarian democracy', in J. Öjendal and A. Dellnäs (eds) *The imperative of good local governance: Challenges for the next decade of decentralization*, Tokyo: United Nations University Press.

Antlov, H., Wetterberg, A. and Dharmawan, L. (2016) 'Village governance, community life and the new Village Law in Indonesia', *Bulletin of Indonesian Economic Studies*, 52(2): 161–183.

Armitage, D., Berkes, F., Dale, A., Kocho-Schellenberg, E. and Patton, E. (2011) 'Co-management and the co-production of knowledge: Learning to adapt in Canada's Arctic', *Global Environmental Change*, 21: 995–1004.

Asian Development Bank (2012) *Indonesia: Water supply and sanitation sector assessment, strategy and road map*, Jakarta: Asian Development Bank.

Aspinall, E. and Mietzner, M. (2010) 'Problems of democratisation in Indonesia: An overview', in E. Aspinall and M. Mietzner (eds) *Problems of democratisation in Indonesia*, pp.1–20, Singapore: Institute of Southeast Asian Studies (ISEAS).

AUSAID (Australian Aid) (2012) *Design document for the Australia–Indonesia Partnership for Pro-Poor Policy: The knowledge sector initiative*, Jakarta: AUSAID.

Bagir, Z. A. (2014) 'Advocacy for religious freedom in democratizing Indonesia', *The Review of Faith & International Affairs*, 12(4): 27–39.

Banks, G. (2009) 'Evidence-based policy making: What is it? How do we get it?' *ANU Public Lecture Series, Productivity Commission*, Canberra, 4 February, https://ssrn.com/abstract=1616460.

Barnes, R. H. (1984) *Whaling off Lembata: The effects of a development project on an Indonesian community*, International Workgroup on Indigenous Affairs (IWGIA) Document 48, Copenhagen: IWGIA.

Bergold, J. and Thomas, S. (2012) 'Participatory research methods: A methodological approach in motion', *Forum: Qualitative Sozialforschung/Forum: Qualitative Social Research*, 13(1) Art. 30, http://nbn-resolving.de/urn:nbn:de:0114-fqs1201302.

REFERENCES

Bievre, D. (2007) 'The question of interest group influence', *International Public Policy*, 27(I): 1–12.

Blair, H. (2000) 'Participation and accountability at the periphery: Democratic local governance in six countries', *World Development*, 28(1): 21–39.

Borang, F., Cornell, A., Grimes, M. and Schuster, C. (2014) 'Bureaucratic politicization and politicized knowledge: Implications for the functioning of democracy', *Conference on the Quality of Government and the Performance of Democracies*, http://qog.pol.gu.se/digitalAssets/1530/1530009_bor--ng--cornell--grimes---schuster.pdf.

Borkman, T. (1976) 'Experiential knowledge: A new concept for the analysis of self-help groups', *Social Science Review*, 50(3): 445–456.

Boyte, H. C. (2004) *Everyday politics: Reconnecting citizens and public life*, Philadelphia, PA: University of Pennsylvania Press.

Bratamihardja, M., Sunito, S. and Kartasubrata, J. (2005) 'Forest management in Java 1975-1999: Towards collaborative management', *ICRAF* (World Forestry Council) *Southeast Asia Working Paper* No. 2005_1 Bogor, Indonesia: ICRAF.

Briggs, J. (2005) 'The use of indigenous knowledge in development: Problems and challenges', *Progress in Development Studies*, 5(2): 99–114.

Brinkerhoff, D. W. and Crosby, B. L. (2001) *Managing policy reform: Concepts and tools for decision-makers in developing and transitioning countries*, Bloomfield, CT: Kumarian Press.

Briner, R. B., Denyer, D., and Rousseau, D. M. (2009) 'Evidence-based management: concept cleanup time?' *Academy of Management Perspectives*, 23(4), 19–32.

Bryant, T. (2002) 'Role of knowledge in public health and health promotion policy change', *Health Promotion International*, 17(1): 89–98.

Bubandt, N. (2014) *Democracy, corruption and the politics of spirits in contemporary Indonesia*, London and New York: Routledge.

Cahyadi, R. (2012) 'Nelayan Dan Pertarungan Terhadap Sumberdaya Laut', *Jurnal Kependudukan Indonesia*, 7(2): 127–144.

Campbell, H. and Marshall, R. (2000) 'Public involvement and planning: Looking beyond the one to the many', *International Planning Studies*, 5(3): 321–344.

Cannadine, D. and Price, S. (eds) (1987) *Rituals of royalty: Power and ceremonial in traditional societies*, Cambridge: Cambridge University Press.

Carden, F. (2009) *Knowledge to policy: Making the most of development research*, New Delhi and Ottawa: Sage and IDRC (International Development Research Centre).

Cartwright, N. and Hardie, J. (2012) *Evidence-based policy: A practical guide to doing it better*, Oxford: Oxford University Press.

Chambers, R. (2012) *Provocations for development*, Rugby: Practical Action Publishing.

Colbran, N. (2010) 'Prosperity denied', *Inside Indonesia*, 13 June, www.insideindonesia.org/prosperity-denied.

Cooke, B. and Kothari, U. (eds) (2001) *Participation: The new tyranny*, London and New York: Zed Books.

Datta, A., Hendytio, M., Perkassa, V. and Basuki, T. (2016) *The acquisition of research knowledge by national-level decision makers in Indonesia*, Jakarta: Knowledge Sector Initiative, www.ksi-indonesia.org/en/news/detail/the-acquisition-of-research-knowledge-by-national-level-decision-makers-in-indonesia.

Denhardt, J. and Denhardt, R. (2007) *The new public service: Serving, not steering* (expanded edn), New York: M.E. Sharpe.

DFAT (Department of Foreign Affairs and Trade) (2015) *Women in Leadership Strategy: Promoting equality and dismantling barriers*, November, Canberra: DFAT, http://dfat.gov.au/about-us/publications/Documents/ women-in-leadership-strategy.pdf.

Durose, C. and Richardson, L. (2016) *Designing public policy for co-production: Theory, practice and change*, Bristol: Policy Press.

Easterly, W. (2015) *The tyranny of experts*, New York: Basic Books.

ELSAM (Lembaga Studi dan Advokasi Masyarakat) (2008) 'Pemantauan terhadap Implementasi Perda-perda Bermasalah', Jakarta, Indonesia: ELSAM, http://lama.elsam.or.id/downloads/1269181690_Tulisan_Monitoring_Perda_-_surur.pdf

REFERENCES

Eyben R., Guijt, I., Roche, C. and Shutt, C. (2015) *The politics of results and evidence*. Rugby: Practical Action Books.

FAO (Food and Agriculture Organization of the United Nations) (2004) 'Building on gender, agrobiodiversity and local knowledge', *Fact Sheet*, Rome: FAO.

FAO (Food and Agriculture Organization of the United Nations) (n.d.) *Challenges to local knowledge*, www.fao.org/tempref/docrep/fao/007/y5631e/y5631e00.pdf.

Fischer, F. (2003) *Reframing public policy: Discursive politics and deliberative practices*, Oxford: Oxford University Press.

Fischer, F. (2009) *Democracy and expertise: Reorienting policy inquiry*, Oxford: Oxford University Press.

Flyvbjerg, B. (1991) *Rationality and power: Democracy in practice*, Chicago, IL: Chicago University Press.

Flyvbjerg, B. (2001) *Making social science matter: Why social inquiry fails and how it can succeed again*, Cambridge: Cambridge University Press.

Fortier, J. (2014) 'Regional hunter-gatherer traditions in South-East Asia', in V. Cummings, P. Jordan and M. Zvelebil (eds) *The Oxford handbook of the archaeology and anthropology of hunter-gatherers*. Oxford: Oxford University Press.

Fung, A. and Wright, E. O. (eds) (2003) *Deepening democracy: Institutional innovations in empowered participatory governance*, London and New York: Verso Press.

Gastil, J. and Levine, P. (2005) *The deliberative democracy handbook: Strategies for effective civic engagement in the twenty-first century*, San Francisco, CA: Jossey-Bass.

Gawande, A. (2016) 'The mistrust of science', *The New Yorker*, June, www.newyorker.com/news/news-desk/the-mistrust-of-science.

Geertz, C. (1973) *The interpretation of cultures: Selected essays*, New York: Basic Books.

Geertz, C. (1983) *Local knowledge: Further essays in interpretive knowledge*, New York: Basic Books.

Gladwell, M. (2002) *The tipping point: How little things can make a big difference*, New York: Back Bay Books.

Gledhill, J. (1994) *Power and its disguises: Anthropological perspectives on politics*, London and Boulder, CO: Pluto Press.

Glover, A. (2015) 'Scientific evidence alone is not what people need or want to inform policy', *The Roberts Lecture 2015*, www.sciencecouncil.org/content/scientific-evidence-alone-not-what-people-need-or-want-inform-policy.

Gorski, P., Kim, D. K., Torpey, J. and Van Antwerpen J. (eds) (2012) *The post-secular question*, New York: New York University Press.

Goss, J. (2000) 'Understanding the "Maluku Wars": Overview of sources of communal conflict and prospects for peace', *Cakalele*, 11 (2000): 7–39, doi: http://hdl.handle.net/10125/426.

Goss, S. (2001) *Making local governance work: Networks, relationships and the management of change*, London: Palgrave.

Grant, C. (2014) 'Politics of knowledge: Whose knowledge matters in trypanosomiasis policy making in Zambia?', *STEPS Working Paper* 73, Brighton: STEPS Centre.

Grenier, L. (1998) *Working with indigenous knowledge*, Ottawa: International Development Research Centre, http://hdrnet.org/214/1/Working_with_indigenous_knowledge.pdf.

Guggenheim, S. (2012) 'Indonesia's quiet springtime: Knowledge, policy and reforms', in A. Reid (ed) *Indonesia rising: The repositioning of Asia's third giant*, Singapore: Institute of Southeast Asian Studies (ISEAS).

Hadiz, V. R. (2003) 'Power and politics in North Sumatra: The uncompleted *reformasi*', in E. Aspinall and G. Fealy (eds) *Local power and politics in Indonesia*, Singapore: Institute of Southeast Asian Studies (ISEAS).

Hall, J. (2003) *Civil Society*, Cambridge: Cambridge University Press.

Hayman, R. and Bartlett, J. (2013) 'Getting to grips with evidence: How NGOs can tackle changing needs in the use of evidence and research', INTRAC (International NGO Training and Research Centre) *Praxis Paper*, November, Oxford: INTRAC.

Heaton, J., Day, J. and Britten, N. (2016) 'Collaborative research and the co-production of knowledge for practice: An illustrative case study', *Implementation Science*, **11**: 20, https://doi.org/10.1186/s13012-016-0383-9.

Hernandez, M. (2012) 'The politics of knowledge in policy analysis', *Pimatisiwin: A Journal of Aboriginal and Indigenous Community Health*, 10(2): 153–160.

Hickey, S. and Mohan, G. (eds) (2004) *Participation: From tyranny to transformation?*, London: Zed Books.

Heryanto, A. (2015) 'Asia literacy: A deeply problematic metaphor', in C. Johnson, V. Mackie and T. Morries-Suzuki (eds) *The social sciences in the Asian century*, Canberra: Australian National University Press.

Holmes, K. and Crossley, M. (2004) 'Whose knowledge, whose values? The contribution of local knowledge to education policy processes: A case study of research development initiatives in the small state of St Lucia', *Compare*, 34(2): 197–214, http://dx.doi.org/10.1080/0305792042000214010.

Hood, C. (1991) 'A public management for all seasons?', *Public Administration Review*, 69(Spring): 3–19.

Hunt, A. and Shackley, S. (1999) 'Reconceiving science and policy', *Minerva*, 37(2): 141–164.

Ibrahim, R., van Tuijl, P. and Antlov, H. (2007) 'NGO governance and accountability in Indonesia: Challenges in a newly democratizing country', in L. Jordan and P. van Tuijl (eds) *NGO accountability: Politics, principles and innovations*, London: EarthScan.

Ichimura, S. (1989) 'A conceptual framework of the political economy of policy-making', in M. Urrutia, S. Ichimura and S. Yukawa (eds) *The political economy of fiscal policy*, Tokyo: The United Nations University.

ICRAF (World Agroforestry Centre) (2014) *Local knowledge*, ICRAF policy guideline series, Jakarta: ICRAF.

Jasanoff, S. (1990) *The fifth branch: Science advisers as policymakers*, Cambridge, MA: Harvard University Press.

Jasanoff, S. (ed) (2004) *States of knowledge: The co-production of science and social order*, London and New York: Routledge.

Jasanoff, S. (2012) *Science and public reason*, London: Earthscan Books.

Jones, H., Jones, N., Shaxson, L. and Walker, D. (2012) *Knowledge, policy and power in international development: A practical guide*, Bristol: Policy Press.

Keefer, P. (2002) 'The political economy of corruption in Indonesia', Washington, DC: World Bank, http://www1.worldbank.org/publicsector/anticorrupt/FlagshipCourse2003/KeeferIndonesia.pdf.

Keesing, R. M. (1991) 'Culture and Asian studies', *Asian Studies Review*, 15(2): 43–50.

Kertzer, D. (1988) *Ritual, politics and power*, New Haven, CT: Yale University Press.

Kingdon, J. (1984) *Agendas, alternatives and public policies*, Boston, MA: Little, Brown & Co.

Kuhn, T. (1962) *The structure of scientific revolutions*, Chicago, IL: University of Chicago Press.

Laaksonen, M. (ed) (2006) 'Local knowledge and international decision-making in development', *KEPA Working Paper* 8, Helsinki: KEPA, www.kepa.fi/tiedostot/julkaisut/local-knowledge.pdf.

Lukes, S. (1974) *Power: A radical view*, London: Macmillan Education.

Mangkusubroto, K., Sarwo Utomo, D. and Ramadhani, D. (2016) 'Supporting decision making for a republic under a complex system', in K. Mangkusubroto, U. Sarjono Putro, S. Novani and K. Kijima (eds) *Systems science for complex policy making: A study of Indonesia*, New York: Springer Publishing.

Manning, C. and van Diermen, P. (eds) (2000) *Indonesia in transition: Social aspects of reformasi and crisis*, Singapore: Indonesia Assessment series, Institute of Southeast Asian Studies,.

Manor, J. (1998) *The political economy of democratic decentralization*, Washington, DC: Direction in Development, World Bank.

Martini, M. (2012) 'Influence of interest groups on policy-making', *U4 expert answer* 335, Bergen, Norway: Transparency International.

Nadasdy, P. (2003) *Hunters and bureaucrats: Power, knowledge and Aboriginal-state relations*, Vancouver: University of British Columbia Press.

Nagy Hesse-Biber, S. (2013) *Feminist research practice: A primer* (2nd edn), London: Sage.

Najam, A. (1995) 'Learning from the literature on policy implementation: A synthesis perspective', *Working Paper* WP-95-61, Vienna: International Institute for Applied Systems Analysis.

Nandy, A. (1989) 'Shamans, savages and the wilderness: On the audibility of dissent and the future of civilizations', *Alternatives*, 14(3): 263–277.

Nasution, A. (2016) 'Government decentralization program in Indonesia', *Asian Development Bank Institute (ADBI) Working Paper* 601, Tokyo: ADBI, www.adb.org/publications/government-decentralization-program-indonesia/.

National Research Council of the National Academies (2012) *Using science as evidence in public policy*, Washington, DC: National Academies Press.

Needham, J. with Wang Ling (1956) *Science and civilization in China, Vol. 1: Introductory orientations*, Cambridge: Cambridge University Press.

Nikijuluw, V. (1998) 'Identification of indigenous coastal fisheries management (ICFM) system in Sulawesi, Maluku and Irian Jaya', *Indonesian Journal of Coastal and Marine Resources Management*, 1(2): 40–51.

Nordic Council of Ministers (2015) *Local knowledge and resource management: On the use of indigenous and local knowledge to document and manage natural resources in the Arctic*, Report of an International Symposium, Copenhagen, Denmark: Nordic Council of Ministers.

Novaczek, I., Harkes, I. H. T., Sopacua, J. and Tatuhey, M. D. D. (2001) *An institutional analysis of Sasi Laut in Maluku, Indonesia*, International Center for Living Aquatic Resources Management Technical Report 59, Copenhagen, Denmark: International Center for Living Aquatic Resources Management.

Nugroho, Y., Prasetiamartati, B. and Ruhanawati, S. (2016) 'Addressing barriers to university research', *Working Paper* 8, Jakarta: Knowledge Sector Initiative.

Ofir, Z., Schwandt, T., Duggan, C. and McLean, R. (2016) *Research quality plus (RQ Plus): A holistic approach to evaluating research*, Ottawa: International Development Research Centre.

Olivier de Sardan, J.-P. (2005) *Anthropology and development: Understanding contemporary social change*, London and New York: Zed Books.

Osborne, D. and Gaebler, T. (1993) *Reinventing government: How the entrepreneurial spirit is transforming the public sector*, New York: Plume Press.

Parkhurst, J. (2017) *The politics of evidence: From evidence-based policy to the good governance of evidence*, Abingdon: Routledge.

Parthasarathy, S. (2011) *Whose knowledge? What values? The comparative politics of patenting life forms in the United States and Europe*, New York: Springer Science+Business Media, LLC.

Patrizi, P. and Quinn Patton, M. (2009) 'Learning from doing: Reflections on IDRC's strategy in action', Ottawa: International Development Research Centre, https://idl-bnc-idrc.dspacedirect.org/handle/10625/47305.

Pawson, R. (2006) *Evidence-based policy: A realist perspective*, London: Sage Publications.

Pellini, A., Alicias, M. D., Nguyen Thi Thu Hang and Permata Bachtiar, P. (2012) 'Technically sound and politically achievable? A taxonomy of knowledge types and their influence on governance in three South-East Asian countries', *Background Note*, London: Overseas Development Institute.

Pimbert, M. (2001) 'Reclaiming our right to power: Some conditions for deliberative democracy', *PLA Notes* 40: *Deliberative democracy and citizen participation*, London: International Institute for Environment and Development.

Pisani, E. and Buehler, M. (2016) 'Why do Indonesian politicians promote Shari'a laws? An analytic framework for Muslim-majority democracies', *Third World Quarterly*, 38(3): 734–752.

Pisani, E., Kok, M. O. and Nugroho, K. (2017) 'Indonesia's road to universal health coverage: A political journey', *Health Policy and Planning*, 32(2): 267–276.

REFERENCES

Pritchett, L., Woolcock, M. and Andrews, M. (2010) 'Capability traps? The mechanisms of persistent implementation failure', Harvard: Kennedy School, www.hks.harvard.edu/fs/lpritch/Governance/capability_traps(june2010).pdf.

Priyono, A. E., Samadhi, W. P. and Törnquist, O., with Birks, T. (2007) *Making democracy meaningful: Problems and options in Indonesia*, Jakarta, Yogyakarta and Singapore: Demos and PCD Press with Institute of Southeast Asian Studies (ISEAS).

Puddy, R. W. and Wilkins, N. (2011) *Understanding evidence, Part I: Best available research evidence. A guide to the continuum of evidence effectiveness*, Atlanta, GA: Centers for Disease Control.

Rakhmani, I. and Siregar, F. (2016) *Reforming research in Indonesia: Policies and practices*, Research Report, Jakarta: Global Development Network.

Reinharz, S. (1992) *Feminism methods in social research*, Oxford: Oxford University Press.

Relph, E. (1976) *Place and placelessness*, London: Pion.

Rose, J. (2017) 'Brexit, Trump, and post-truth politics', *Public Integrity*, (19: 555–558, www.tandfonline.com/doi/full/10.1080/10999922.2017.1285540.

Russo, J. (2012) 'Survivor-controlled research: A new foundation for thinking about psychiatry and mental health', *Forum: Qualitative Sozialforschung/Forum: Qualitative Social Research*, 13(1), Art. 8, http://nbn-resolving.de/urn:nbn:de:0114-fqs120187.

Said, E. (1978) *Orientalism*, New York: Vintage Books.

Sandel, M. J. (2012) *What money can't buy: The moral limits of markets*, New York: Farrar, Straus and Giroux.

Sandercock, L. (1998) *Making the invisible visible: A multicultural planning history*, Berkeley, CA: University of California Press.

Schaffer, F. (1998) *Democracy in translation: Understanding politics in an unfamiliar culture*, Ithaca, NY: Cornell University Press.

Scott, J. (1998) *Seeing like a state: How certain schemes to improve the human condition have failed*, New Haven, CT: Yale University Press.

Seamon, D. and Sowers, J. (2008) 'Key texts', in P. Hubbard, R. Kitchen and G. Vallentine (eds) *Human Geography*, 2008, pp. 43–51, London: Sage.

Sen, A. (1999) *Development as freedom*, New York: Knopf.

Simpson, H., de Loë, R. and Andrey, J. (2015) 'Vernacular knowledge and water management: Towards the integration of expert science and local knowledge in Ontario, Canada', *Water Alternatives*, 8(3): 352–372.

Siregar, P. R. and Crane, T. A. (2011) 'Climate information and agricultural practice in adaptation to climate variability: The case of climate field schools in Indramayu, Indonesia', *CAFÉ*, 33: 55–69, doi:10.1111/j.2153-9561.2011.01050.x.

Sjamsuddin, H. (2016) 'Dinamika Sosial Urang Banjar dalam Sejarah', Antasari Islamic State University, Banjarmasin, http://idr.uin-antasari.ac.id/6218/1/Dinamika%20Sosial%20Urang%20Banjar%20dalam%20Sejarah.pdf.

Spencer, J. (2007) *Anthropology, politics and the state: Democracy and violence in South Asia*, Cambridge: Cambridge University Press.

Stokes, D. (1997) *Pasteur's quadrant: Basic science and technological innovation*, Washington, DC: Brookings Institution Press.

Suiter, J. (2016) 'Post-truth politics', *Political Insight*, 7(3): 25–27.

Surowiecki, J. (2004) *The wisdom of crowds: Why the many are smarter than the few*, New York: Random House.

Suryawan, I. N. (2017) *Papua versus Papua: Perubahan dan perpecahan budaya*, Yogyakarta: LABIRIN.

Susskind, L. E. and Cruikshank, J. L. (2006) *Breaking Robert's rules: The new way to run your meeting, build consensus and get results*, Oxford: Oxford University Press.

Taleb, N. N. (2010) *The bed of Procrustes: Philosophical and practical aphorisms*, New York: Random House.

Tengö, M., Brondizio, E. S., Elmqvist, T., Malmer, P. and Spierenburg, M. (2014) 'Connecting diverse knowledge systems for enhanced ecosystem governance: The multiple evidence base approach', *Ambio*, 43(5): 579–591, Sweden: Stockholm Resilience Centre, Stockholm University.

Thaman, R., Lyver, P., Mpande, R., Perez, E., Cariño, J. and Takeuchi, K. (eds) (2013) *The contribution of indigenous and local knowledge systems to IPBES: Building synergies with science*, IPBES (Intergovernmental Science-Policy Platform on Biodiversity and Ecosystem Services) Expert Meeting Report, UNESCO/UNU, Paris: UNESCO, http://unesdoc.unesco.org/images/0022/002252/225242E.pdf.

Törnquist, O. (2002) *Popular development and democracy: Case studies with rural dimensions in the Philippines, Indonesia and Kerala*, Oslo: Centre for Development and the Environment, University of Oslo.

Tuhiwai Smith, L. (1999) *Decolonizing methodologies: Research and indigenous people*, London: Zed Books.

University of York (2012) *The co-production of knowledge*, York: Science and Technology Studies Unit, University of York, www.york.ac.uk/media/satsu/events-docs-images-media/publication.pdf.

Van Klinken, G. (2000) 'What caused the Ambon violence?', *Inside Indonesia*, 60, www.insideindonesia.org/what-caused-the-ambon-violence.

Von Benda-Beckmann, F., von Benda-Beckmann, K. and Brouwer, A. H. (1992) 'Changing "indigenous environmental law" in the Central Moluccas: Communal regulation and privatization of sasi', Paper presented to the *Congress of the Commission on Folk Law and Legal Pluralism* at Victoria University, Wellington, August.

Vincent, J. (1990) *Anthropology and politics: Visions, traditions, trends*, Tucson, AZ and London: The University of Arizona Press.

Weiler, H. (2009) 'Whose knowledge matters? Development and the politics of knowledge', in H. Theodor, H. N. Weiler and H. Dickow (eds) *Festschrift for Peter Molt: Entwicklung als Beruf*, pp. 485–496, Baden-Baden: Nomos, http://web.stanford.edu/~weiler/Texts09/Weiler_Molt_09.pdf.

Weiss, C. H. (1979) 'The many meanings of research utilization', *Public Administration Review* 39(5): 426–431.

Weiss, C. H. (1997) *Evaluation* (2nd edn), Upper Saddle River, NJ: Prentice-Hall.

WHO (World Health Organization) (2013) 'WHO traditional medicine strategy, 2014–2023', Geneva: WHO, http://apps.who.int/iris/bitstream/10665/92455/1/9789241506090_eng.pdf?ua=1.

Wildavsky, A. and Pressman, J. L. (1973) *Implementation: How great expectations in Washington are dashed in Oakland; or, why it's amazing that federal programs work at all*, Los Angeles, CA: University of California Press.

Wood, N. (2006) *Transmitting craft knowledge: Designing interactive media to support tacit skills learning*, Doctoral thesis, University of Sheffield Hallam.

Yanow, D. (2003) 'Accessing local knowledge', in M. Hajer and H. Wagenaar (eds) *Deliberative policy analysis: Understanding governance in the network society*, pp. 228–246, Cambridge: Cambridge University Press.

Yearley, S. (2000) 'Making systematic sense of public discontents with expert knowledge: Two analytical approaches and a case study', *Public Understanding of Science*, 9: 105–22.

Zimmerman, T. (n.d.) *Tacit knowledge in post-bureaucratic organizations*, www.academia.edu/2101565/Tacit_Knowledge_in_Post_Bureaucratic_Organizations.

Zinnbauer, D. (2009) 'The role of investors in strengthening corporate integrity and responsibility', in D. Zinnbauer, R. Dobson and K. Despota (eds) *Global corruption report: Corruption and the private sector*, Transparency International, Cambridge University Press, Ernst & Young. New York: Cambridge University Press, https://transparency.hu/wp-content/uploads/2009/09/Global-Corruption-Report-2009-final-eng.pdf.

Index

Note: Page numbers followed by n indicate footnotes. Page numbers in *italics* indicate figures and tables.

A

academic research 1–3, 11–14, 17
  see also scientific knowledge
Aceh Besar
  Keujruen Blang (resource-sharing mechanism) 78–80, 91–92
  mawah (traditional financing and investment mechanism) 81–82, 99–100, 109–110, 111–112, 128–129
  tsunami 93
  Water User Farmer Associations (P3A) 79–80, 91, 105
activism 23–24
advocacy knowledge 29, 33–34
advocacy organisations 38–39, 40
  see also LAHA (Institute for HIV/AIDS Advocacy)
AIDS *see LAHA* (Institute for HIV/AIDS Advocacy)
anthropology 44, 92, 101
Antlov, H. 22, 24, 55
Aristotle 32
Armitage, D. 17
Artha Wacana Christian University (*Universitas Kristen Artha Wacana*) 96
audience priority 144

B

Banjarmasin 73–75, 96–98, 105–106, 117, 133
Banks, G. 10, 40, 147, 150
Bau Nyale (folk festival) 67
Baumata Timur 60–63
  see also Pikul Association (*Perkumpulan Pikul*)
Beng Mawah Micro-Finance Institution 82, 122–123
BIGS (Bandung Institute for Governance Studies) 5, 41, 75–78, 101, *102*, 113–114, 123–124
  inclusion 123–124
  language 113, 114
Blaikie, P. 116
budgeting 23, 122
bureaucracy 121, 145
bureaucratic knowledge 22, 29, 33–34, 35–36, 42
bureaucratic power 46–48

C

Carden, F. 8, 57
case studies
  map of locations 7
  summary 4–5
  see also individual case studies

cattle 81
Centers for Disease Control 139–140
Centre for Anthropological Studies, University of Indonesia (PUSKA UI) *see* PUSKA UI (Centre for Anthropological Studies, University of Indonesia)
Centre for Education and Community Studies (PKPM) *see* PKPM (Centre for Education and Community Studies)
Centre for Politics and Government, Gadjah Made University (POLGOV UGM) *see* POLGOV UGM (Centre for Politics and Government, Gadjah Made University)
Centre for Regional Studies and Information (PATTIRO), Jakarta *see* PATTIRO (Centre for Regional Studies and Information)
citizen activism 23–24
citizen knowledge 18, 146
see also local knowledge
citizen organisations 43
citizen participation / involvement 47, 53–57, 123, 147
see also community participation
citizen perception 23
citizens 31
civil service 21, 21n
civil society 18
civil society coalitions 108
civil society networks 84–85
civil society organisations 2n, 18, 23, 27, 56, 108–108, 130, 134
see also non-governmental organisation
climate change 4, 33, 65–69, 92, 95, 113–114
codification 37–38, 41, 106–111

co-evolution 38n, 92
co-governance 47–48
commercialisation 117–118
common knowledge 37, 103, 106
communication 119–127
community forests 76–78, 101
community participation 53–57, 134–137, 144
see also citizen participation / involvement
Community-based Drinking Water and Sanitation Provision Programme (*Penyadiaan Air Minum dan Sanitasi Berbasis Masyarakat (PAMSIMAS)*) 60–63, 92
cooperatives 83, 100
co-production 17–18, 30, 38–41, 141–142, 144, 149
see also knowledge: interaction between forms of
craft knowledge 36n
see also local knowledge
credibility 14, 15
cultural representations 44
cultural studies 44

D

Datta, A. 22, 23
decentralisation 2, 21, 22–23, 24, 49, 55
deliberative democracy 47
democratisation 2, 53, 54–55, 56, 57, 146
Denhardt, J. and Denhardt, D. 46–47.
de-professionalisation 56, 146–147
development planning 23, 47, 53, 122–123
disaster 117
disaster response 52
discrimination 134
distributive justice 137

diversity 31, 40, 113–114
donors 50–51
Drinking Water and Environmental Health Working Group (*Pokja AMPL*) 63
Drucker, P. 57
Durose, C. 39

E

East Lombok 66–67, 68, 69, 125–126
East Nusa Tenggara
 influence 130
 mining 83–85, 116–117, 148
 water management 60–63, 92, 117, 123, 132
 whale fishing 50, 63–65, 117–118, 126
economic cooperation *see mawah* (traditional financing and investment mechanism)
economic development 50–51
economic shocks 117–118
El Niño 65–66
electoral assets 132–134
empowerment 55
enabling environment 147
environment 92–94
environmental change 116, 117
 see also climate change
episteme 32
ethnocentrism 11
evidence 2, 13, 19, 20, 46, 139–140
 see also knowledge; local knowledge
evidence-based management 12–13
evidence-based policy 18–19
experiential knowledge 36, 36n
 see also local knowledge

F

faith *see* religious knowledge
farmer schools (*Penyuluh Pertanian Papangan (PPL)*) 67–68
financial cooperation *see mawah* (traditional financing and investment mechanism)
fishing *see* whale fishing
fishing regulations *(sasi lompa)* 4, 69–72, 93–94, 98, 99, 107
Food and Agricultural Organization (FAO) 36–37, 103–104, 106
Forest Circle Society Network 83
forest conservation 5, 76–78, 101, 113
formal scientific knowledge *see* scientific knowledge
Foundation for People's Welfare (YKU) *see* YKU (Foundation for People's Welfare)

G

Geertz, C. 41, 44
gender 17, 38, 40, 50, 53, 65, 104–106, 118, 140
governance 13, 53–57
 see also co-governance
Grenier, L. 37
Guggenheim, S. 20–21

H

Hadiz, V. 24
Haruku island 69–72, 93–94
health insurance 5, 85–88, 89–90, 98, 112, 135, 137
hegemonic knowledge 109
Heryanto, A. 15, 99
HIV/AIDS advocacy *see LAHA* (Institute for HIV/AIDS Advocacy)
human rights 134

I

identities 100
indigenous practices 38
Indonesian Academy of Sciences (AIPI) 21–22
Indonesian Institute of Sciences (LIPI) 98
Indramayu 66–67, 68–69, 95, 113–114, 125–126
influence 127–130
  relationship-based 130–132
Institute for HIV/AIDS Advocacy, Kendari *see* LAHA (Institute for HIV/AIDS Advocacy)
Institute for Islamic and Society Studies (LK3) *see* LK3 (Institute for Islamic and Society Studies)
interest groups 48–50, 49n
intermediary knowledge 29, 33–34
International Development Research Centre (IDRC) 14–15
isomorphic mimicry 10

K

Kendal 76–78, 124
Kendari 85–88
keuchik 78n, 81, 128
Keujruen Blang (resource-sharing mechanism) 5, 49, 78–80, 90–92, 130, 133
knowledge
  historical relationship between policy making and 46–48
  interaction between forms of 95–98, 142, 143, 150. *see also* co-production
  and power 15, 17
  tensions between different types of 143–146
  typology 11–14, *12*, 29–30, 32–39, 103, 140
  see also local knowledge

knowledge assets 148–151
knowledge hierarchies 14–20, *16*
knowledge sector 2, 2n, 20–22
Knowledge Sector Initiative (KSI) xi, 2–3, 2–3n, 59
knowledge systems 38
knowledge-to-policy process 6–10, *8*, *9*, 150
  local knowledge in 22–24, 40–41, 103
  politics of 130–137
Kolhua Dam 61
Konawe Selatan 85–90, 112, 128
Kuhn, T. 32n

L

LAHA (Institute for HIV/AIDS Advocacy) 5, 85–88, 89–90, 112, 135
Lamalera 63–65, 63n, 115–116, 126
language 113–114, 121
legitimacy 122
Lembaga Advokasi HIV/AIDS (LAHA) (Institute for HIV/AIDS Advocacy) *see* LAHA (Institute for HIV/AIDS Advocacy)
Lembata island 50, 63–65, 104, 114–116, 117–118, 126, 137
linguistic diversity 113–114
LK3 (Institute for Islamic and Society Studies) 4, 73–75, 96–98, 105–106, 133
local innovation 38
local knowledge 12, 13–14, 36–39
  as an asset 148–151
  codification 37–38, 41, 106–111
  communication of 119–127
  definitions 3, 44
  as electoral asset 132–134
  generation 89–92
  inequalities 17, 103, 118

INDEX

interaction with local environment 92–94
locality and origin 98–101
management 111–116
and participatory development 53–56
in policy making 22–24, 48–50, 140–141, 142–143
political-economy dimensions 44–46, 103–106
sources of xi, 145–146
strategic role 146–147
tensions between other forms of knowledge and 143–146
local knowledge actors 107–108
local knowledge reproduction 120
local politics 24, 130
local sentiment 122
local wisdom 145–146
locality 128
Lukes, Stephen 41

M

manganese ore exploitation *see* mining
Manggarai 83–85, 107–108
Martapura river 73–75
Masehi Injili Church, Timor 96
mawah (traditional financing and investment mechanism) 5, 81–82, 98, 99–100, 109–110, 111–112, 122–123, 128–129
meaning 44
melesi (sharing tradition) 85–88, 89–90, 98, 112, 128, 137
Merangan forest 76–78
micro-finance *see mawah* (traditional financing and investment mechanism)
migration 66, 68, 116–117, 141–142
mining 5, 83–85, 103, 108, 130, 136, 148

Mintzberg, H. 36
motivation 123
Muhammadiyah Disaster Management Centre (MDMC) 52
Musrenbang (development planning forum) 123
see also development planning
myths 62, 74, 113

N

National Medium-Term Development Plan (RPJMN) 2015-2019 vii–viii
new public management 46–47
new public service 47
non-governmental organisations (NGOs) 18, 26, 59n, 68, 83, 103
see also civil society organisations
Nordic Council of Ministers 13
Nugroho, K. 24

P

Pancasila 51
Papua 10–11, 98
Parkhurst, J. 9, 13
parliament (incl. local) 24, 75, 121–122, 131–133
participatory development 53–57
see also citizen participation / involvement; community participation
PATTIRO (Centre for Regional Studies and Information) 4, 69–72, 93–94, 107, 108, 131–132
Pellini, A. 46
Penyadiaan Air Minum dan Sanitasi Berbasis Masyarakat (PAMSIMAS) (Community-based Drinking Water and Sanitation Programme) 60–63, 92

Penyuluh Pertanian Papangan (PPL) (farmer schools) 67–68
Perkumpulan Petani Pemakai Air (P3A) (Water User Farmer Association) 79–80, 91, 105
Perkumpulan Pikul (Pikul Association) *see* Pikul Association (*Perkumpulan Pikul*)
phronesis 32
physical environment 92–94
Pidie 82
Pikul Association (*Perkumpulan Pikul*) 4, 60–63, 148
  academic community 96
  communication 120
  interaction with local environment 92
  language 114
  local knowledge as electoral asset 132
  modernisation 94
PKPM (Centre for Education and Community Studies) 5, 78–80, 91–92
  communication 121–122
  influence 131
  local knowledge as electoral asset 133
  religious groups 130
  women 105
place 100–101
Pokja AMPL (Drinking Water and Environmental Health Working Group) 63
POLGOV UGM (Centre for Politics and Government, Gadjah Made University) 5, 83–85, 103
  community forums 136
  community participation 134
  data collection 110–111
  local actors 107–108, 130
  local knowledge as electoral asset 132–133

popular education 129
policy advocacy 121–122, 130
  see also advocacy organisations
policy entrepreneurs 39
policy implementation 10, 47, 134–137
policy legitimacy 122
policy making
  historical relationship between knowledge and 46–48
  influence on 127–132
  and local knowledge 48–50, 119–127
  types of knowledge in 30–31
policy processes *see* knowledge-to-policy process
policy reform 10
policy research institutes 40
  see also think tanks
political-economy perspective 44–46, 103–106
politics 19, 44–46
popular education 129
population growth 116
Poros Photo 4, 63–65, 116, 126–127
post-truth politics 18–19
power 41, 45
  bureaucratic 46–48
  devolution of. *see* decentralisation
  interest groups 49–50
  and knowledge 15, 17
pranata mangsa (farming calendar) 65–66, 66n
Pressman, J.L. 47
problem definition 144–145
professional knowledge 12, 29, 33–36, 40, 42, 140
profit sharing system *see mawah* (traditional financing and investment mechanism)
Programme for International Student Assessment (PISA) 15n

INDEX

public administration 20–21
public decision making 46–48
public management 46–47
public policy making *see* policy making
PUSKA UI (Centre for Anthropological Studies, University of Indonesia) 4, 65–69
  codification 108–109
  communication 124–126
  community participation 135–136
  influence 127–128, 131
  interaction between forms of knowledge 95
  interaction with local environment 92
  outreach 148

R

rainfall 65–69, 95, 125–126
relationship-based influence 130–132
religion 70, 70n, 84, 129–130
religious institutions 107–108
religious knowledge 50–52, 74, 96–98
research methodology 14
rice fields 90–92
Richardson, L. 39
river conservation 4, 73–75, 97–98, 105–106, 133

S

sasi lompa (fishing regulations) 4, 69–72, 93–94, 98, 99, 107
science field shops *(Warung Ilmiah Lapangan)* 68–69, 92, 95, 124, 125
scientific community 96
scientific knowledge 8, 14, 32–33, 34, 42, 140
  communication of 124–126
  limitations 11, 150
  and local context 56
scientific rigour 144
secularisation 50
shared knowledge 37, 103, 106–107
Sirius Labs 126
Smith, T. 11, 147
social relevance 15
socio-cultural context 111–113, 126
socio-economic change 116–117
socio-economic perspective 45
Southeast Sulawesi 85–88, 89–90, 112, 118, 128, 137, 146
specialised knowledge 37, 103
Spencer, J. 44
stakeholders 108
Suharto 20, 24
Susuk Wangan ceremony 77–78

T

techne 32
technical evidence 46
think tanks 21, 29, 33–34, 34
Timor island *see* Pikul Association *(Perkumpulan Pikul)*
Torong Besi 83–85, 123, 148
tourism 64, 115–116, 137, 150
tsunamis 93, 117

U

units of analysis 145
units of impact 145
Universitas Kristen Artha Wacana (Artha Wacana Christian University) 96
universities 17, 21, 40, 127
  Artha Wacana Christian University *(Universitas Kristen Artha Wacana)* 96

see also POLGOV UGM (Centre for Politics and Government, Gadjah Made University); PUSKA UI (Centre for Anthropological Studies, University of Indonesia)

V

values 114–115
Village Law No.6/2014 22–23, 80

W

water management 4, 60–63, 92, 120, 123, 132, 148
Water User Farmer Associations (P3A) 79–80, 91, 105
whale fishing 4, 50, 63–65, 104, 114–116, 117–118, 126, 150
Wildavsky, A. 47
women 50, 105–106
  see also gender
Women in Leadership Strategy (DFAT, 2015) 40

Y

YKU (Foundation for People's Welfare) 5, 81–82, 99–100, 109–110, 122–123, 128–129

Z

Zimmerman, T. 35